TAMA FORTNER

GO Bible™

KNOW, GROW, and GO

90 Devotions on Gospel Transformation for Kids

TYNDALE KIDS™
Tyndale House Publishers
Carol Stream, Illinois

FEATURING THE
new living TRANSLATION

Visit Tyndale's website for kids at tyndale.com/kids.

Know, Grow, and Go: 90 Devotions on Gospel Transformation for Kids

Designed by Jacqueline L. Nuñez

For manufacturing information regarding this product, please call 1-855-277-9400.

For information about special discounts for bulk purchases, please contact Tyndale House Publishers at csresponse@tyndale.com, or call 1-855-277-9400.

ISBN 979-8-4005-1543-9

Printed in China

32 31 30 29 28 27 26
7 6 5 4 3 2 1

Introduction

Hello, and welcome to *Know, Grow, and Go*!

In these pages, you'll find ninety devotions based on the truths of the Bible, from Genesis to Revelation. These devotions are written to be read and discussed as a family, but you can do them on your own if you prefer. Each devotion begins with a verse—because what could be better than starting with God's Word? The devotions themselves are packed with true-to-life stories and examples, along with Bible stories and facts to help you KNOW who God is, how much he loves you, and how much he wants to be in your life.

And that's just the beginning. Because while faith starts with knowing God, it definitely doesn't end there! That's why each devotion is followed by five sections designed to help you GROW in your faith and then GO share it with the people around you. Check these out:

Read All About It gives you the exact chapters and verses in the Bible you need to dig a little deeper and get to know God's Word even better.

Talk About It offers conversation starters to use around the kitchen table, in the car, or during family devotion time. If you're not reading this devotional with your family, you can think through them on your own. These questions will not only spark discussions, but they'll also help you take the devotions to the next level and apply them to your own life.

Pray About It leads you through a prayer and connects you with the God who is always listening, always wanting to talk to you, and always ready to help.

Let's Do This is all about applying God's Word to your life and the situations you face. It might be a quick, no-supplies-needed activity. Or it might simply be a question or two to challenge the way you think about God, yourself, and others.

Go Bigger is, well, bigger. These activities are for when you have a little more time and the desire to really put God's Word to work in your life. It might be a family activity or a game. It might be an outreach idea. Or it might be a Bible-based challenge. No matter what it is, Go Bigger is your opportunity to put your faith into action!

As you read through these devotions, my prayer is that the title will become truth in your life—that you will come to **KNOW** God and his great big love for you even better, that your faith in him will **GROW** bigger and bolder each day, and that you will then take that love, knowledge, and faith and **GO** share it with the world!

With love,
Tama

1

Looking and Loving Like God

God created human beings in his own image. In the image of God he created them; male and female he created them.

GENESIS 1:27

From stars and starfish to meerkats and the mountains on the moon, God created *everything*! But out of all the things in his creation, only one is created in his image: people. Only *we* are made to look like him.

Does that mean you have the same color eyes or hair as God? Or that you stand as tall as he does, or that he has freckles like you? No, not exactly. What it *does* mean is that you are made to "look" like God in the thoughts you think, the words you say, and the things you do. In other words, you are made to give, and serve, and love like God.

Will that be easy? Not always. Will you do it right every time? Nope! Only Jesus could do that.

Looking like God doesn't just happen either. Learning to give, serve, and love like him takes practice. *Lots* and *lots* of practice. It's something you'll work on your whole life through.

The good news is that God will help you look more and more like him. He's given you his Word, the Bible, to guide you. And even better? When you decide to follow him, he'll send his own Holy Spirit to live inside you and help you.

Why did God create you to look like him? Because that way you can go out into the world and show others what he looks like. After all, they were made in his image, and he wants them to look more and more like him too.

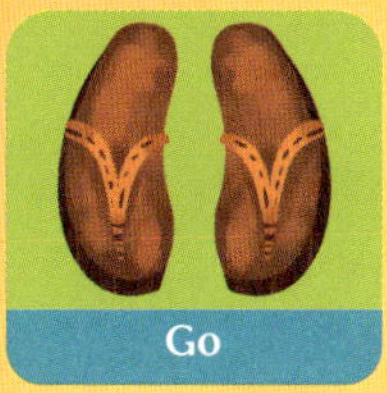

Read All About It

Read more about how God created people in Genesis 1:26-2:23.

Talk About It

Have you ever been hanging out with a friend and then suddenly found yourself talking, or sitting, or laughing like them?

We all do it! We start to look and act like the people we spend time with. So what do you think will happen when you spend time hanging out with God?

Pray About It

God, we thank you for making us in your image. Help us to look more and more like you. We want our words and our actions to show the world what you look like—the God who loves them. Amen.

Let's Do This

Ask God to remind you that *everyone* (yes, that person too!) is created in his image and endlessly loved by him. Next time you're annoyed or frustrated with someone, think of a few ways that person looks like God.

Go Bigger

As a family, choose a verse that will help you love others the way God loves them, and memorize it. But don't stop there! Make it your mission to live out that verse this week. Together, brainstorm ways to do that.

Not sure which verse to pick? Try Matthew 25:35, Ephesians 4:32, or 1 Thessalonians 5:11.

2

Feeling Invisible?

You are the God who sees me.

GENESIS 16:13

Do you ever feel invisible—and not in that cool, superhero kind of way? Sometimes it can seem like people are just too busy to notice you. Like everyone and everything else are more important. Like no one sees you at all.

That's about how Hagar felt. She was Abram and Sarai's servant—before they became Abraham and Sarah. And it's kind of a long story, but she was also about to be the mother of Abram's child. That made her mistress, Sarai, angry. *Really angry.* Sarai was so horrible to Hagar that she ran away.

Hagar believed no one cared about what she thought or what she wanted. She was scared and alone in the wilderness with no one to help her. It was like she was invisible.

But Hagar wasn't invisible. Not to God. He saw her *and* he sent his angel to help her. Because that's what God does. He sees, and he helps.

God doesn't just see long-ago people of the Bible. He doesn't just see the popular or the "perfect" people either. God sees *everyone*. You know what that means, right? He sees *you* too.

You are *never* invisible to God. He always knows what you're going through. He sees when you win and when you miss the winning shot. He sees when you try to do what's right, but it all turns out wrong. He knows when you don't know what to do.

God sees, and he knows, and he comes to help you.

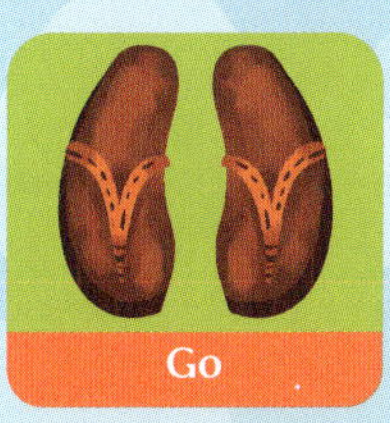

Read All About It

Read more about how God saw Hagar in Genesis 16:1-14.

Talk About It

When God looks at the earth, he doesn't just see a huge group of people. Instead, he *chooses* to see each and every individual person. He sees you. He knows your name. He knows what you had for breakfast. What does this tell you about God's power? About God's heart?

Pray About It

God, you have so many people and so many things to keep an eye on. Yet you still choose to see and watch over each one of us. That's amazing! Thank you for loving us like that. Amen.

Let's Do This

God sees everyone. It's one of the ways he shows that he cares. Follow God's example today and show that you care by *seeing* the people around you. Look them in the eye and smile. If you know their name, say it. Let them know they are important enough to be seen by you.

Go Bigger

Who's the invisible person in your life? Who gets left out of conversations and picked last for the team? Who doesn't get invited . . . to anything? Have you thought of someone?

Go and talk to them, choose them for your team, invite them to hang out with you and your friends. Be the person who sees them.

3

Trust God to Bless You

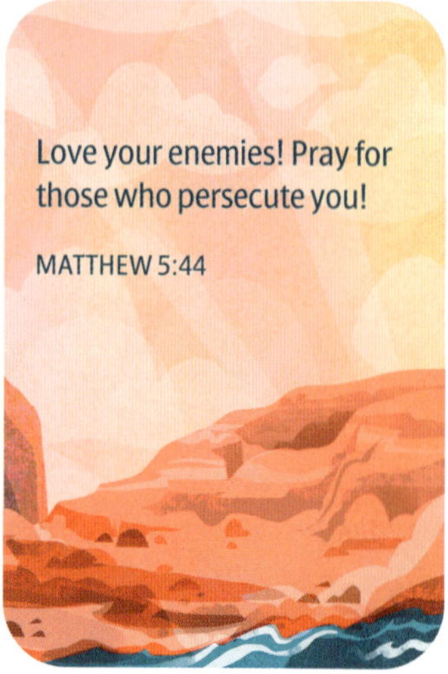

Every once in a while, you'll bump into someone who just seems to enjoy being mean. You might be tempted to bully them right back.

That's probably what Isaac, Abraham's son, was tempted to do. He was all grown up and had a family of his own when a famine struck. He moved his entire household to the land of the Philistines in search of food and water. Scary, right? But God gave Isaac a promise: "I will be with you and bless you" (Genesis 26:3). God kept his promise in a big way!

Isaac's crops and herds of animals grew bigger and better than ever before. His success made the Philistines jealous, though. And their jealousy made them mean. They filled up Isaac's wells with dirt, and their king threw him out of the country!

Three times, Isaac moved and dug new wells. Three times his enemies took them from him. Isaac and his servants dug one last well. This time, no one tried to take it away. God had made a place for him.

Isaac chose peace instead of anger, arguing, or fighting back. He trusted God to bless him, just as he promised.

When someone is unkind or even just plain mean, you might be tempted to argue or fight back. But that would be acting *more* like them and *less* like God. Instead, take a deep breath and ask God what you should do. That might be simply walking away, or it might mean finding a grown-up to help you. Trust God to find a way to bless you.

Read All About It

Read more about how Isaac trusted God to bring peace in Genesis 26:12-33.

Talk About It

When you're faced with a bully or someone who just isn't very nice, you have choices to make. Talk about some times when it's best to choose to walk away, when you need to stand up for yourself (or someone else), and when you need to ask for help.

Pray About It

God, when we feel pushed around and bullied, help us to know what to do and say—and what *not* to do and say. Remind us that you will make a way to bless us. Amen.

Let's Do This

You know that person who's not so nice? The one who likes to bully and push others around? Talking to them might not be the safest or most fun thing to do, but you can pray for them. Ask God to change their heart and help them learn to love their neighbors too.

Go Bigger

God made a space for Isaac to live in peace. You and your friends can do the same in your neighborhood or school. Band together and decide to be a safe space for other kids where no one gets picked on or laughed at. Pray for each other, be kind, and cheer each other on.

4

A Change of Heart

I will give you a new heart, and I will put a new spirit in you. I will take out your stony, stubborn heart and give you a tender, responsive heart.

EZEKIEL 36:26

Have you ever said to yourself, *That person will never change! He'll always be a cheater. She never tells the truth. Once a snob, always a snob.* So you don't even try to be their friend. You don't include them in your prayers. Basically, you give up on them.

God doesn't do that. *Not ever.*

Not even with this guy named Judah.

Judah was one of the ten brothers who attacked their younger brother Joseph. They were all jealous of Joseph and angry with him. When they saw their chance, they grabbed him and threw him into a pit. Judah and his brothers even planned to kill Joseph—that is, until Judah saw a way to make some money off his brother. He talked his other brothers into selling Joseph as a slave.

Judah was definitely not a nice guy. In fact, he was pretty terrible. But God didn't give up on him. He used the things that happened later in Judah's life to change his heart. Judah changed so much that, years later, he was ready to become a slave himself in order to save his brother Benjamin.

God is an expert at taking the people we think are hopeless and changing them for the good. He might even use *you* to help change their hearts!

(PS: Just in case you're wondering . . . God never gives up on you either!)

Read All About It

Read more about Judah's change from bad guy to hero in Genesis 37:23-28 and Genesis 44:18-33.

Talk About It

God doesn't give up on people. When people choose to do bad or hurtful things, he doesn't walk away. Instead, God works in their lives to help them change and become the people he created them to be. Why is that a good thing for everyone—including *us*?

Pray About It

God, please change our hearts and help us to love all people, not just those who are easy to love. Show us how we can point them to you. Amen.

Let's Do This

Do something nice today for someone who isn't so easy to be nice to. Perhaps it's a grumpy neighbor, a difficult classmate, or that brother or sister you're just a little bit upset with right now. (And don't forget: The nicest thing you can ever do is pray for someone.)

Go Bigger

This world gives up on people too easily. But we can be different. Find a place where you as a family can volunteer to help those who are struggling. It might be a homeless shelter, a food bank, or even an animal rescue. Let God work through you to make a difference in someone else's life.

Listen and Love

My sheep listen to my voice; I know them, and they follow me.

JOHN 10:27

What would happen if your teacher said, "Turn in your homework," but you didn't listen? You'd end up with a bad grade, right? That bad grade is an example of a *consequence*.

When we choose not to listen to teachers or parents or other wise authority figures in our lives, we receive consequences. But when we choose not to listen to God, those consequences are really not pleasant. Just ask Pharaoh.

In Bible times, Pharaoh was the title of Egypt's ruler. The Pharaoh in Exodus was cruel, and he forced God's people to be his slaves and build his cities. When the people cried out for help, God heard them. He sent Moses to give Pharaoh a message: "Let my people go" (Exodus 5:1).

Pharaoh refused to listen, and the consequences were plagues of frogs, boils, locusts, darkness, and worse! There were ten terrible plagues. All because Pharaoh refused to listen.

When we don't listen to what God tells us in the Bible, we may experience some yucky consequences too. (Probably not frogs or boils, though. *Whew!*) It's not because God wants to punish us, but because God loves us. *Huh?* You see, God loves us so much that he wants to help us do what's good and right. He uses consequences to teach us to love and listen to him.

Because when we *do* listen to him, God helps us through the hard times. He helps us find joy and peace. And he helps us learn more and more about him. The more we learn about him, the more reasons we'll find to love him.

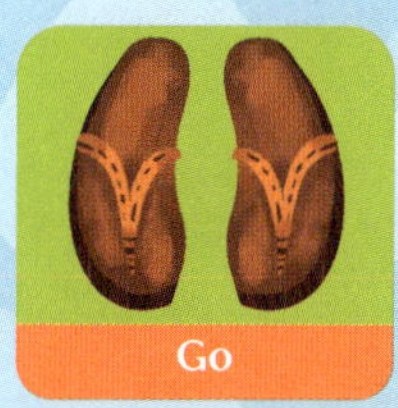

Read All About It

Read more about the first plague in Exodus 7. Then read what Jesus says about listening in John 10:1-16.

Talk About It

Listening is more than just hearing what someone says and doing it. It sends a message. Listening to someone tells them they're important enough for us to stop what we're doing and pay attention to them. What does that say about why God wants us to listen to him? What does it say about God wanting to listen to us?

Pray About It

God, we don't want to miss one single thing you have to say to us. Help us turn away from distractions, and help us to listen to you. And please forgive us when we don't. Amen.

Let's Do This

Practice listening to the people around you, and not just with your ears. Listen with your whole body. How? Look the other person in the eye. Lean in and get just a little closer. Ask questions, and don't interrupt. Repeat what they say to make sure you understand.

Go Bigger

Practice listening with a Sound Scavenger Hunt. Create a list of ten sounds to listen for around your home. They might include things like a barking dog, a passing car, a ticking clock, a humming refrigerator, or an airplane flying overhead. Set a timer and race to see who can identify the most sounds.

6

No Problem Too Big

As you grow up and learn to do new things, you might start to think you can take care of yourself. Sometimes that's true. Chances are, you can fix simple, everyday problems like tying your shoelace when it comes undone or making a snack when you're hungry.

There will be times, though, when something comes along that's so big you can't handle it on your own. The good news is, nothing's too big for God. No challenge, no trouble, no problem. God can handle it all! He can do big and impossible-for-us things. Like the way he helped the Israelites cross the Red Sea.

It was just after God's people had escaped from slavery in Egypt. Pharaoh changed his mind about letting them go and decided he wanted his slaves back. So he sent his army charging after them! The Israelites were trapped, with Pharaoh's army behind them and the Red Sea stretching out in front of them.

The Israelites called out to God to rescue them . . . *and he did!* Did God send a boat? No! Did he tell the Israelites to swim for it? No! God split the Red Sea right in two, and the Israelites strolled across the now-dry bottom of the sea. *Amazing!*

Here's a wonderful thing you need to know about God: It doesn't matter how big or small your trouble is. You can tell him about it and trust him to help you. Let him show you the big and impossible things he can do for you.

Read All About It

Read more about how God made a way through the Red Sea in Exodus 14.

Talk About It

God can do big, huge, wonderful, and amazing things! Like splitting a sea in two, stopping a storm, and making a blind person see. But did you know there are two things God will never do? He will not lie or break a promise (see Numbers 23:19 and Hebrews 6:18). Talk about what that means for you and his promises to you.

Pray About It

God, you do things we could never even dream of doing. Open our eyes today to see just a little bit of how huge, marvelous, and amazing you are! Amen.

Let's Do This

Step outside and find a place to stand. Slowly turn in a circle and let your eyes fill up with all the things God has created—things no one else could ever make, like the sky and trees and butterflies. How many can you name?

Go Bigger

Sometimes God answers prayers in ways that are obviously miraculous. Other times, he uses us to answer someone's prayer. It can be as simple as being a friend.

As a family, identify someone from your church who isn't able to get out of the house and invite them into your family circle. Encourage them by taking them a meal, playing a game with them, or simply visiting for a while.

7

No Leftovers, Please!

> Seek the Kingdom of God above all else, and live righteously, and he will give you everything you need.
>
> MATTHEW 6:33

Imagine looking forward to your favorite dinner. Then, when you walk in, everyone else has already eaten. There's nothing left but a few crumbs! That's kind of what it's like when you put God last in your life and just give him your leftover time and attention.

Maybe you think, *I'll talk to God after I hang out with my friends,* but then you're too tired to pray. Or you might think, *I'll give God the money that's left after I buy that game,* but then you only have a few cents left.

God doesn't want the leftovers of your time, and he doesn't want the crumbs of your giving. God wants the best of you—your heart, your time, and your giving.

That's one reason why God gave the Israelites so many instructions about how to worship him.

Some of those instructions were about what the priests would wear. They couldn't just wear any old robe and sandals. Their clothing had to be specially made in just the way God said. It also had to be worn in just the way God said. It had to be *the best.* Not because God cares so much about clothes. But because this helped the people remember how important it was to bring their best to God.

When you're tempted to give God the leftovers of your day, remember that God gave you his very best: Jesus. Then ask yourself—and ask him—*How can I give God my best today?*

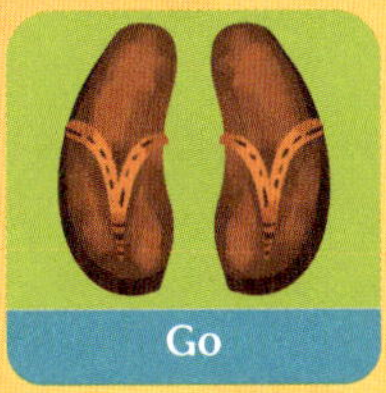

Read All About It

Read more about the special clothing for the priests in Exodus 28.

Talk About It

God wants more than our leftovers. He wants our best. What would it look like to give God the leftovers of our time, and our money and things, and our heart? Now think about it the opposite way: What would it look like to give him the best of our time, our money and things, and our heart?

Pray About It

God, please forgive us when we give you our leftovers. Teach us how to give you the best of all we have . . . our time, our stuff, and especially our hearts. Amen.

Let's Do This

Psalm 46:10 says, "Be still, and know that I am God!" One way to put God first is to spend time with him. Set aside time today to simply sit with him and to declare in your heart that he is God!

Go Bigger

Give God the best of your time by setting aside a family Sabbath. Choose a day and time that works for your family. (Hint: It doesn't have to be all day or even Sunday.) Do things like prepare and share a meal together. Pray. Sing songs. Read a favorite verse or story from the Bible. Take turns sharing the gifts from God you are most grateful for. Turn off all the noise and screens, and give God the best of you.

8

When You Need a Second Chance

> Return to the LORD your God, for he is merciful and compassionate, slow to get angry and filled with unfailing love.
>
> JOEL 2:13

Why do we do things we shouldn't do? Sometimes it's to make ourselves happy. We might even be a little (or a lot!) selfish about it. Other times, we might do something because we're sad. Or we might say something because we're angry . . . and then later wish we hadn't.

But God is different. Every single thing God does begins and ends with love. Like what he did for the Israelites after he rescued them from slavery in Egypt.

The Israelites were on their way to the Promised Land when God called Moses up to the top of Mount Sinai. While Moses was busy talking to God, the Israelites were busy too. Not busy doing good things. No, they were busy forgetting about God and all he had done to save them. They even made a calf-shaped idol out of gold and started worshiping it.

God was very angry. He could have said, *I'm done with these people!* Or found another group to be his people. But he didn't.

Instead, God gave them another gift. He gave them mercy. He gave them a second chance to love, follow, and obey him.

God didn't give the Israelites mercy because they were so awesome. And he didn't give them a second chance because they deserved it. God did it because he loved them.

Everything God does is because of his huge and never-ending love for us. Stick with him, and he'll teach you to do everything out of love too.

Read All About It

Read more about God's great love and mercy in Exodus 34:1-11.

Talk About It

We all mess up. We all sin. We all deserve God's anger, just like those Israelites did. But instead of anger, God gives us mercy. He gives us another chance to do the right thing. Why? Because he loves us. Talk about the gift of mercy and why we all need it so much.

Pray About It

Lord, please forgive us when we get too busy and forget about you. Thank you for all the second chances you give us to love and follow and worship you. Amen.

Let's Do This

God would love to see you give mercy to the people around you. Be on the lookout today for someone who needs the gift of a second chance—and then give it to them. Not because they deserve it, but because that's what God does for you.

Go Bigger

When we forget about God, that's when the trouble starts. To help you remember, make a "remember bracelet." Grab a piece of string or leather cord. Add beads, if you like. Tie it around your wrist. (Keep it loose. Not too tight!) Every time you see it, remember God and whisper, *Thank you for loving me.*

9

The Center of Everything

When you wake up in the morning, what's the first thing you think of? When you're daydreaming, what pops into your mind? And when it's time to close your eyes at night, what thoughts do you think? Chances are that those thoughts are about the things that are most important to you. They're like the center of your life.

That's where God wants to be. Right smack in the middle of your thoughts—and the middle of your life.

That's where God wanted to be for the Israelites too. He used the Tabernacle to teach them this truth.

The Tabernacle was a huge tent. Blue, purple, and scarlet curtains made up the Tabernacle's walls. These curtains hung on frames of acacia wood set in silver bases and held together with clasps of bronze. Light poured out from a golden lampstand. This was definitely *not* like any tent you would go camping in. This tent was fit for a king . . . the King of all creation!

It was here, inside the Tabernacle, that God came down to meet with Moses. And it was where the Israelites worshiped God.

Wherever they went, the Israelites carried the Tabernacle with them. And whenever they stopped to camp, they set up the Tabernacle in the center of all their tents. Why? So that every time they saw it—which was often—the Israelites would remember that God should be the center of their whole lives.

How can you make God the center of your life? Turn to him with every question, every need, and every thank-you and praise. Turn to him with everything!

Read All About It

Read more about the Israelites and the Tabernacle in Numbers 2.

Talk About It

God wants to be at the center of everything we do and say and think. But what does that look like on an ordinary Tuesday? At breakfast? At work or school? At games and at practices? At bedtime? Talk about ways your family can make God the center of your lives.

Pray About It

God, you are huge and mighty and more powerful than we could ever imagine. And yet you choose to love and care for us. Help us to thank you by making you the center of everything we think and say and do. Amen.

Let's Do This

Psalm 139:17-18 says that God's thoughts about you can't even be counted! They're more than the grains of sand on all the seashores in the whole world! Think about that today, and let yourself smile . . . because God is thinking about you.

Go Bigger

The kitchen is often the "heart," or center, of the home. Pick a spot—perhaps at the kitchen table—and make a space for God. Add a Bible, devotional book, and maybe a way to play worship music. Whenever you gather there, take a moment to invite God into the center of your thoughts and life.

Different Like Him

> You must be holy in everything you do, just as God who chose you is holy.
>
> 1 PETER 1:15

God is holy. There isn't a single speck of sin, evil, or darkness in him. He is good, pure, and perfect—and different from anything in this world. And God wants you to be holy too.

Wait! What? God wants you to be holy—to be perfect—like him? But that's just not possible, is it? You can be pretty good when you decide to be. But you can't be perfectly perfect every single second of the day—no one can! What are you going to do?

Don't worry.

God knows you aren't perfect. He understands you'll make mistakes. But you *can* still be different from the world around you. And he'll be right there to help you.

In Old Testament times, God gave his people laws to follow. These laws helped them to be holy—different from the world around them. When they sinned, God's laws told them how to make sacrifices to pay for those sins.

But then Jesus came and sacrificed himself to pay for *all* our sins and make us holy. Forever! Even better, when you choose to follow Jesus, God sends his very own Holy Spirit to live inside you. He'll help you choose what is good and pure and right.

Of course, in a world where so many people choose to do wrong, you'll stand out. Will that be easy? No. Sometimes it'll be really hard. People might laugh or refuse to be your friend. But God won't be laughing. He'll be cheering you on when you choose to be different like him.

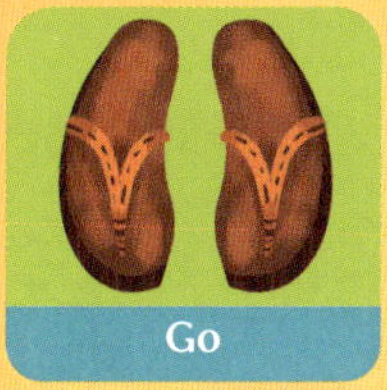

Read All About It

Read more about how God expects his people to be holy in Numbers 5:5-8 and Romans 12:1-2.

Talk About It

When God asks us to stand out from the crowd, he doesn't mean wearing wild clothes or acting weird. Instead, he asks us to love him in a world that would rather forget him. How can you show others how much you love God? How can you do it with your words *and* without saying a word?

Pray About It

Father God, you are holy and good and perfect in every way. Please help us to be just a little bit more like you each and every day. Amen.

Let's Do This

Look for ways to be holy today. Be different, and stand out from the crowd in the best of ways. How? Pick a fruit of the Spirit (check out Galatians 5:22-23) and decide to live it out every chance you get today.

Go Bigger

One of the greatest ways to be different for God is to live out the fruit of the Spirit. Gather and prepare a few different kinds of fruit, and place them in nine cups or bowls. Label each with a different fruit of the Spirit. As you share the snack with your family, brainstorm ways you can live out that fruit in your own lives—and then go do it!

11

Grumble! Mumble! Rumble!

Grumble! Mumble! Rumble! What is that? It's not the sound of a train. And it's not the sound of your stomach hungry for an after-school snack. It's the sound of whining, complaining, and arguing. It's also the sound the Israelites made as they tromped through the wilderness.

The Israelites had a problem with mumbling and grumbling. A pretty big one. God had done so much for them, and they weren't even grateful. Whenever their leaders—Moses and his brother Aaron—told them to do something they didn't want to do, they complained and argued. *Grumble! Mumble! Rumble!*

One day, God decided to prove that Moses and Aaron really were his chosen leaders. He sent the twelve leaders of Israel's tribes—including Aaron—to get their staffs. Moses placed them inside the Tabernacle. The next morning, Aaron's staff was blooming. That old, dry, dead piece of wood had even grown almonds! Not in days or weeks, but in just one night. Aaron's blooming staff was a reminder to the people that they needed to stop mumbling and grumbling and be grateful for all God was doing for them.

God gives us reminders too. Every tree, every squirrel, every cloud in the sky is a reminder of the amazing things he can do.

The next time you feel like whining or complaining or arguing, take a look around. Let God's creation remind you of all the reasons you have to be thankful—and all the reasons you have to praise him.

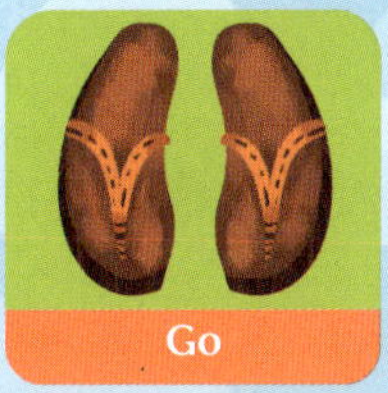

Read All About It

Read more about how Aaron's staff burst into bloom in Numbers 17:1-11.

Talk About It

When we mumble, grumble, whine, and complain, it's often because we don't want to do something we need to do. When are you most likely to argue and complain? How can you turn that "I *have* to do this" attitude into a grateful "I *get* to do this" attitude?

Pray About It

God, when we're tempted to whine, complain, or even argue, please change our hearts. Open our eyes to see all the reasons we have to smile and say thanks to you. Amen.

Let's Do This

Make today a "No Mumble and No Grumble" day. Every time you catch yourself mumbling or grumbling or even arguing about something you don't want to do, stop and name three things you're grateful for instead.

Go Bigger

Turn that "No Mumble and No Grumble" day into a week for the whole family. Start by hanging a big piece of paper on the refrigerator. Every time someone stops to name three things they're thankful for, write them on the paper. At the end of the week, read them off and praise God for all the good things he's given you.

12

Always with You

Come to me with your ears wide open. Listen, and you will find life.

ISAIAH 55:3

Want to know something amazing? God is constantly sending you messages to let you know he's with you. Like sunrises every morning. Like popping just the right Bible verse into your thoughts, or sending a friend when you need one most. Or stopping your donkey in the middle of the road.

Okay, that last one probably won't happen to you. But it did happen to a guy named Balaam. He and his donkey had set off to meet with Israel's enemies. They'd promised Balaam lots of money if he would curse God's people. Of course, God wasn't happy about this, and he sent an angel to stop him. Balaam couldn't see the angel, but his donkey could!

First, the donkey ran away. Next, it stomped on Balaam's foot. Finally, the animal lay down in the middle of the road. Balaam was so furious he started hitting the donkey with his staff.

That's when things really got interesting. The donkey spoke up and said something like, "Why are you hitting me? Have I ever done this kind of thing before?"

"No," Balaam said. (He was so angry he didn't realize he was talking to a donkey!)

At that moment, God opened Balaam's eyes, and he saw the angel holding a sword, ready to stop him. Balaam realized the donkey had saved him. It was God's way of sending him a message.

God sends you messages all the time. But when you're busy thinking about yourself and what you want, you can miss them. Don't wait for a donkey to tell you. Ask God to open your eyes—and help you see every message he sends.

Read All About It

Read more about Balaam and his donkey in Numbers 22:21-35.

Talk About It

When God has a message for you, he keeps repeating it until you understand. It took Balaam's donkey three tries—and a miraculous conversation!—to get Balaam's attention. How can you get better at listening to God and his messages through quiet time, prayer, and reading the Bible?

Pray About It

God, help us not to be like Balaam. Open our ears and our hearts to all that you want to tell us. Amen.

Let's Do This

We can get so busy thinking about the past or worrying about the future. But it's in this present moment that God speaks to us. Take a few minutes today to simply stop, look, and listen to the world around you. Where do you see that God is with you and working in your world?

Go Bigger

One of the ways God speaks to us is through his Word, the Bible. Gather together as a family and choose a passage to read. (The Sermon on the Mount in Matthew 5–7 is a great one to start with.) As you listen, share the words and phrases that jump out at you most. What is God's Word telling you?

Little Changes

> Trust in the LORD with all your heart; do not depend on your own understanding. Seek his will in all you do, and he will show you which path to take.
>
> PROVERBS 3:5-6

The Israelites were headed for the Promised Land at last. It had been a long, long, *long* journey for them—about forty years longer than it should have been. That's because the Israelites struggled to trust the God who had rescued them from Egypt.

But God didn't waste that long journey. He used the time with his people to show them who he was and that he could be trusted. He protected them from enemies, fed them with manna and quail, and made sure they had water in the desert wilderness. He even made sure their shoes didn't wear out! Step by step, the Israelites learned to follow God. Not perfectly. But better than before.

Your life is a little like that journey. You're traveling through the wilderness of this world with God. As you spend time with him—talking to him and studying his Word—he'll teach you more and more about who he is. He'll show you that you can trust him to protect you and give you the things you need.

Knowing and trusting God changes you. Not all at once, but a little at a time. Sometimes the changes are so small, you might think you're not changing at all—until you stop and look back at where you started. For example, a year ago, if someone made you mad, you might have tried to get even. Now, you might ask God to help you forgive them instead.

Those little changes are like steps in the journey that you and God will travel together your whole life through.

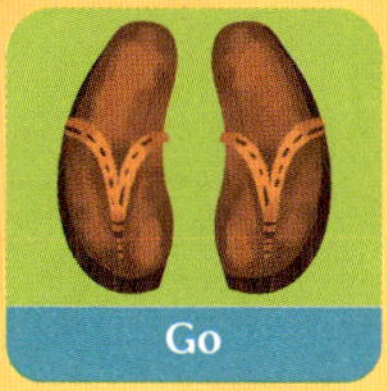

Read All About It
Read more about the Israelites' long journey in Numbers 33:1-48.

Talk About It
Learning to follow God and live how he wants us to is a lesson we'll be learning our entire lives. Take turns sharing a way you've learned to trust God and how he's helped you.

Pray About It
God, thank you for walking with us through every day of our lives. Please help us to love and trust you more today than we did yesterday. Amen.

Let's Do This
Look back through pictures of when you were younger. How much have you grown since then? Try to remember what you knew about God when you were three, five, and seven years old. How much better do you know him now?

Go Bigger
To help you remember to follow God every step of the way, play an epic game of Follow the Leader. Start at home and then follow your leader through your neighborhood. Along the way, add in fun ways to share God's love, such as holding open a door or waving hello to a neighbor. Be sure to take turns being the leader.

14

God Will Fight for You

[God] led me to a place of safety; he rescued me because he delights in me.

PSALM 18:19

The Israelites were under attack! King Og of Bashan and his *entire army* were after them. The Israelites might have been a little worried, but God wasn't. Not one bit. He already knew what he was going to do.

"Do not be afraid of him," God told his people. "I have given you victory over Og and his entire army" (Deuteronomy 3:2).

Did you see that? Did you notice what God said? He said he had given his people the victory *before* he did it. God knew he could and would defeat that army. And that's exactly what he did. He fought for his people.

When you're facing a problem that's just too big, when the enemy is too tough, and when you don't have a clue what to do, remember this fact: God fights for his people.

God doesn't just toss you out into the world and say, "Good luck! I hope everything turns out okay." No!

When you trust God to take care of you, he will shield you and guide you. He will tell you when to move forward and when to be still. And when you need him to, God will fight for you.

God already knows the perfect way to rescue you. And when you see *how* he rescues you, you'll discover that you can trust him no matter how big the battle is. All you have to do is ask.

(PS: God wants to help you with all your little battles too.)

Read All About It

Read more about how God fought for his people in Deuteronomy 3:1-22.

Talk About It

God is both *omniscient* and *omnipresent*. Those great big "omni" words mean that God knows everything and has always been in every place and time—past, present, and future. What would being omniscient and omnipresent be like? What does God's omniscience and omnipresence mean for your life and his promises to you?

Pray About It

Lord, you already know every trouble and every struggle we'll ever face. And you also already know the perfect answers. Help us trust you to shield us, guide us, and fight for us. Amen.

Let's Do This

You probably aren't going to be chased down by an enemy army today. But you might feel attacked—by unkind words, troubles, or just a rough day. Before you jump in and fight back, ask God to show you what to do. He'll have the perfect answer.

Go Bigger

Just how big is God (endless) and how much does he know (everything)? To get an idea of the power of God, gather as a family and spend some time looking up photos taken from space, such as those from the Hubble Space Telescope. Talk about how the God who is big enough to create all that heavenly beauty is ready to fight for you.

15

The Most Important Things

> The LORD is the everlasting God, the Creator of all the earth. He never grows weak or weary. No one can measure the depths of his understanding.
>
> ISAIAH 40:28

No one is born knowing everything. We have to learn. And we learn things at different ages and stages. For example, when you were a toddler, you learned to walk and talk. When you got a little older, you learned to tie your shoes and read a book. But those driving lessons will probably have to wait a few years.

There are some lessons, though, that God wants even the youngest children to learn—like the truth about who he is.

So, who is God?

- He is the creator of this world and everything in it (Genesis 1:1).
- He is the creator of you (Psalm 139:13).
- He will watch over you (Psalm 121:8).
- He will listen to you and help you (Psalm 34:17).
- He loves you so much that he sent his own Son to save you (John 3:16).

In the Bible, God gives special instructions for kids just like you. Why? Because you matter to him. And because he wants you to grow up knowing how much he loves you and that he'll always be there to rescue you.

Learning about God doesn't stop when you're a kid, though. There's so much more to learn—more than you could ever know. And that's a wonderful thing. Because it means you get to spend your whole life learning more and more about God and his great big, endless love for you!

Read All About It

Read more about teaching God's commands to children in Deuteronomy 6:4-9.

Talk About It

God, the Creator of the entire universe, knows each of us inside and out. And what's even more amazing is that he wants each of us to know him. He wants a relationship with us. Talk about what a relationship is and some of the different kinds, like friend to friend and parent to child. How incredible is it that God wants to have a relationship with you?

Pray About It

Father God, we will never know everything there is to know about you. But we know what matters most: that you love us and that we love you. Amen.

Let's Do This

Deuteronomy 6:7 says to talk about God and his commands "when you are at home and when you are on the road, when you are going to bed and when you are getting up." Make it your mission to do that today—and try to do it every day. Talk—or think—about God wherever you are and wherever you go!

Go Bigger

In Deuteronomy 6:9, God tells his people to write his commands on the doorways to their homes. Have each family member write a favorite Bible verse or promise on heavy paper or cardboard. Bonus points if you make it look like a street sign. Then have each person post it at the doorway to their room.

16

You Can't Outgive God

God doesn't *need* anything from us, but he wants us to give to him out of joy and thankfulness for everything he's done.

In the Old Testament, God taught his people to tithe as one way of doing that. Tithing means giving ten percent to God. For example, if your allowance is ten dollars, you would tithe—or give—one dollar to God. (Since you can't exactly hand God money, you can give it to your church or to an organization teaching his Word or helping his people.)

By the time Jesus came to earth, though, some of the religious leaders had gotten very picky about tithing. Oh, they gave one tenth of their money and crops—but not one smidgen more! Check out what Jesus said about that: "Give, and you will receive. Your gift will return to you in full—pressed down, shaken together to make room for more, running over, and poured into your lap. The amount you give will determine the amount you get back" (Luke 6:38).

The truth is, even though the religious leaders were giving their tithes, their hearts were stingy and full of greed. They gave, but they weren't happy about it.

Everything we have is a gift from God. *Everything*: our money, our stuff, our time, and even our talents. We're not really giving our things to God. We're just returning part of what he gave us, so there's no need to be stingy. When we give cheerfully and with thankful hearts, we'll quickly find that we can't outgive God. (Though he loves to see us try!)

Read All About It

Read more about giving in Deuteronomy 14:22-29, Luke 6:38, and 2 Corinthians 9:7-8.

Talk About It

Luke 6:38 comes right after verses that talk about giving love (v. 35), compassion (v. 36), and forgiveness (v. 37). Could it be that God wants us to give not only our money and our things, but also our love, compassion, forgiveness, time, and talents (see 1 Peter 4:10)? How can you give each of these things back to God?

Pray About It

Father God, our lives are so rich with all the gifts you've given us. Open our eyes to see every one of them, and open our hearts to share them with others. Amen.

Let's Do This

Since you're young, you may not have much money to give. But you do have smiles, prayers, and praises. How many smiles can you give away today? How many people can you pray for? And how many things can you find to praise God for today?

Go Bigger

Why not tithe your time this weekend? Since there are forty-eight hours in a Saturday and Sunday, a tithe would be about five hours. How could you and your family give your time? Perhaps it's helping with a church project, volunteering for a community cleanup, or hosting a meal for newcomers to your church. How can you give back to God?

Who Do You See?

If you help the poor, you are lending to the LORD—and he will repay you!

PROVERBS 19:17

God loves his people and cares about how they are treated and what happens to them. Not just some people or on some days—he loves and cares about all people at all times. But God especially keeps watch over the poor, the helpless, and those who can't speak up for themselves.

Now, the Israelites had been slaves for hundreds of years. They knew how slaves were treated, and they knew how slave owners were treated. But God wanted his people to be different. So when the Israelites headed into the Promised Land, God gave them laws about how to love and care for each other. Those laws included things like leaving part of their crops in the fields for the poor to harvest. Jesus summed up all these laws in Matthew 22:39 with one simple command: "Love your neighbor as yourself."

In our world today—just like in Bible times—some people are treated like they don't matter. Maybe it's because they're poor or alone or sick. But every person matters to God. He's still keeping watch over everyone. He protects those who can't protect themselves. He helps those who need help. He sees the people no one else notices or cares about. God wants you to do the same. Why? Because God protects, helps, and cares about you. The best way to thank him is to try to love others the way he loves you.

Read All About It

Read more about how God cares for all people in Deuteronomy 24:17-22.

Talk About It

All through the Bible—from the Old Testament to the New Testament—God tells us to take care of his people. Especially those who cannot help themselves. How is loving and caring for others a way to love and worship God?

Pray About It

Lord, we confess that sometimes we choose not to see the people in need around us. Please forgive us. Teach our hearts to *want* to care for others, and guide us to those who need our help. Amen.

Let's Do This

Sometimes it seems so much easier to look away or just keep walking when we see someone who needs help. Like that kid who always seems to "forget" their lunch, but, in reality, their family doesn't always have enough money to buy food. Today, pack an extra snack for school and find someone to share it with.

Go Bigger

Some of the easiest people to "not see" are the homeless. Prepare help kits for them by tucking socks, snacks, a bottle of water, a Bible verse, and an encouraging note into a plastic bag. Keep them handy in the car so you're ready to help when you see someone in need. Or make it a family mission for the day to drive around and give away as many kits—and prayers—as you can!

18

When You Don't Understand

This is my command—be strong and courageous! Do not be afraid or discouraged. For the LORD your God is with you wherever you go.

JOSHUA 1:9

At last! After forty years of wandering in the wilderness, it was time for the Israelites to march into the Promised Land. It wasn't going to be easy. There were battles to fight and enemies to defeat. The first one was the mighty city of Jericho with its stone walls that soared up so high and wrapped around the entire city.

Joshua had taken Moses' place as leader of the Israelites. He trusted God to help them fight and win against Jericho. And Joshua was ready to fight. But when God came to him with the battle plan, it wasn't what Joshua expected. *March around the city? For six days?* Then on the seventh day, God said, "March around the town seven times, with the priests blowing the horns. When . . . the priests give one long blast on the rams' horns, have all the people shout as loud as they can" (Joshua 6:5). Then the walls of Jericho would fall down.

Ummm . . . Blow trumpets? Shout?

God's plan didn't make a whole lot of sense to Joshua. But he followed that confusing plazn anyway, and it worked! Why? Because it was God's plan.

Sometimes God will ask you to do things you don't understand. Like help someone but don't tell them it was you, or forgive instead of getting even. In the world's eyes, that kind of thing doesn't make sense. But our job isn't to fully understand God—that's impossible anyway! Our job is to obey him and trust him to work everything out. Because he always will.

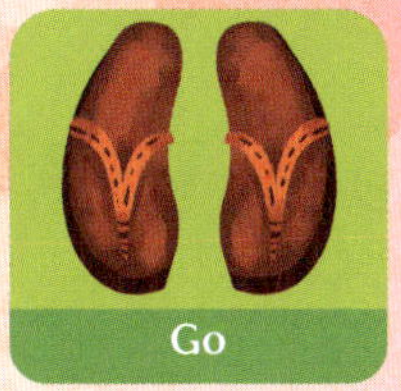

Read All About It

Read more about God's defeat of Jericho in Joshua 6:1-20.

Talk About It

God's commands don't always make sense in this world. Like "Love your enemies" and "Forgive those who hurt you." Why do you think God asks us to do these things? How might they help us draw closer to God?

Pray About It

God, we humans like to understand everything, but you're just too amazing to completely understand. Help us to trust and follow you, especially when we don't understand. Amen.

Let's Do This

Is there something you know you need to do, but you don't want to? Maybe it's saying you're sorry or forgiving a friend. Maybe it's stepping out and leading a prayer or a Bible study. Ask God to help you want to do it—and to give you the courage to do it.

Go Bigger

Is there a story or a part of the Bible you don't understand? Is there one of God's commands you struggle to follow, or a promise that doesn't quite make sense? Gather as a family and read the passage together. Ask God to open your heart to what he means. Look it up in a Bible dictionary or commentary. Ask your pastor or a trusted adult to help you.

19

Get the Facts First

> The LORD doesn't see things the way you see them. People judge by outward appearance, but the LORD looks at the heart.
>
> 1 SAMUEL 16:7

***Why is she cutting line** in the lunchroom? Why's that guy digging through the trash?* When others do things we think they shouldn't, it's easy to decide they're up to no good.

That's what some Israelites thought about other Israelites who were in different tribes. You see, after the Israelites moved into the Promised Land, each of the twelve tribes went to their own part of the land. The land for Reuben, Gad, and half of Manasseh's tribe, though, was on the opposite side of the Jordan River from the other tribes. Near the river, they built an altar.

When the other Israelite tribes heard about the altar, they thought those two-and-a-half tribes were worshiping a false god. They were furious! They rounded up their army and weapons and prepared to attack.

Fortunately, they sent over a few men to talk first. They discovered that the two-and-a-half tribes had built the altar to remind themselves of how great and mighty God was. They also didn't want any other Israelites to forget that they were God's people too—even though they lived on the other side of the river.

Instead of rushing to judge, stop and take a closer look. Have a conversation. Because what if that girl cutting line is helping a friend on crutches who can't carry her food? What if that guy is digging through the trash because he dropped something in there—or he's hungry? Don't hurry to decide others are doing wrong. Get the facts and make sure you know what's really going on.

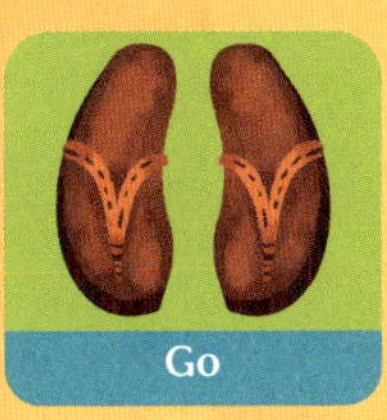

Read All About It

Read more about the importance of being slow to judge in Joshua 22:10-34.

Talk About It

There are two kinds of judging in the Bible. One is deciding someone is bad and doesn't deserve grace (see Matthew 7:1-2). But only God knows what's going on in people's hearts. And the truth is, no one deserves grace—it's a free gift! The other kind of judging is good for us to do, though. It's also called "discerning," and it means looking at someone's actions and deciding if you should follow their example (see Matthew 7:15-20). What makes that kind of judging good?

Pray About It

Lord, you are the perfect judge. Only you can see inside our hearts. Help us not to try to steal your job away. Amen.

Let's Do This

The next time you catch yourself judging someone's actions, stop and ask God to help you see what's really going on.

Go Bigger

One of the best ways to learn not to unfairly judge others is to "walk in their shoes." That means trying to understand what they're doing from their point of view. Give this idea a fun twist by putting a pair of everyone's shoes in a pile. At "Go!" have everyone race to put on two shoes—any shoes—and then run to a finish line.

20

The Secret to Leading

The Bible is full of stories about how God used men and women to lead his people and do his work. One of those people was a woman named Deborah.

Deborah was both a judge and a prophet of God. The people often came to her with their questions and disagreements. She was a strong leader. The people listened to Deborah and followed her because they knew she listened to God.

At the time Deborah led Israel, the Canaanites were their enemies. Sisera, the Canaanite leader, was incredibly cruel. He had 900 iron chariots at his command, and he used them to terrorize the Israelites. When the people cried out for help, God spoke to Deborah. She listened carefully as God told her exactly how and when to attack Sisera.

Deborah then called for Barak, the commander of Israel's army, and told him the plan. Barak agreed to go to battle, but *only* if Deborah went with him. So guess what? She did! Sisera's huge army was defeated that day, just as God had promised.

Deborah knew the secret to being a good leader: Listen to God and have a heart that is willing to do what he says. That's also the secret to being a follower of God. When you do those things, God will give you the victory too.

Read All About It

Read more about Deborah in Judges 4–5.

Talk About It

In Matthew 20:25-28, Jesus talked about what it means to be a good leader. Read those verses together. How does Jesus say we should lead? (Hint: It's not about being the boss!) What might it look like for a leader to put themself last?

Pray About It

Lord, when you offer us a chance to step out and lead, remind us that the best leaders are those who serve others. Amen.

Let's Do This

If you want to lead like Jesus, you have to remember that it's not about being in charge. It's about serving others and leading by example. Look for an opportunity to lead by serving today. It could be helping the teacher or a friend, picking up trash, or simply choosing to be kind.

Go Bigger

Leading like Jesus means leading by example. Play this mirror game as a fun way to practice leading by example. Have two people stand facing each other. One will be the leader and the other will be the mirror. The leader will move their arms, legs, head, and fingers, and the mirror will try to copy them. How silly can you get? How fast can you go?

21

Stay Alert!

> The temptations in your life are no different from what others experience. And God is faithful. He will not allow the temptation to be more than you can stand. When you are tempted, he will show you a way out.
>
> 1 CORINTHIANS 10:13

When God first spoke to Gideon, he was hiding down in a winepress to thresh out his wheat to make it edible. Why? Because Midianite raiders would regularly steal the Israelites' food. So Gideon hid . . . until God found him, that is.

God took that unlikely guy and made him a great leader. With God's help, Gideon tore down idols, defeated the Midianites' huge army with only 300 men, and brought peace to the land. The Israelites were so relieved that they wanted to make Gideon their ruler. He quickly said, "No thanks. The Lord is your ruler." Gideon did ask for one thing, though . . .

He asked for each person to give him one gold earring from the treasures they had taken from their enemies—which they happily did.

What Gideon did with those earrings was not good. It was not good at all! He melted them down and made an idol. Soon Gideon and all the people were worshiping it like it was a god!

That's what Gideon did. But what did Gideon *not* do? Check with God! Gideon was feeling so puffed up over the victory and everyone loving him that he forgot it was only possible because of God.

Here's the thing: It's okay to be tempted. Everyone is tempted by something—even Jesus was tempted (see Matthew 4:1-11). You might be tempted by pride like Gideon was. Or it might be greed, gossip, or lying that tempts you. Stay alert and don't give in! Ask God to help you spot those temptations and say no to them.

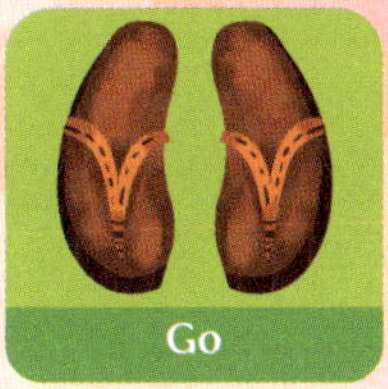

Read All About It

Read more about Gideon's victory and his big mistake in Judges 6–8.

Talk About It

Everything was going right for Gideon. Then he let down his guard, and the devil slipped in with a temptation. When are you most tempted to do wrong? Is it when everything is going your way? When you're tired or hungry? When you're trying to fit in? How can you stay strong and resist temptation?

Pray About It

Lord, when we are tempted, help us to see right away that the thing we want to do isn't good or right. And please show us how to stay far away from that sin. Amen.

Let's Do This

For the next week, keep a record of when you're tempted to do wrong. What tempted you? What was going on that made it harder to say no? Brainstorm ways to avoid this temptation in the future. For example, get a good night's sleep, keep a healthy snack handy, or don't hang out with a certain group.

Go Bigger

Play this twist on the Floor Is Lava game. First, brainstorm five or more temptations, such as lying to get out of trouble or gossiping. Take turns calling out a temptation, followed by "The floor is lava!" Everyone then has five seconds to run away from temptation and find a safe place off the floor.

All for Who?

God has given each of you a gift from his great variety of spiritual gifts. Use them well to serve one another.

1 PETER 4:10

Have you heard of Samson from the Bible? He was the super huge guy with the super long hair and superhuman strength.

Samson's strength was a gift from God. He had so many chances to use his strength to help the Israelite people and to show them how awesome God is. But did he? No! Samson used his gift of strength to destroy, to hurt others, and to take what he wanted. And let's just say things didn't end very well for Samson.

God's gifted you in important ways too. You might know exactly how you're gifted, or you might still be figuring it out. The real question is, *What are you going to do with your gift?*

Are you going to be selfish like Samson and use your gift just for yourself? Or will you use it to help others and tell them about God?

For example, if you can hit all the notes in every song, will you set out to be the star of every show or will you help others learn to sing praises to God? If you're a soccer ace, will you hog the ball and try to score all the goals, or will you help your teammates do their best too?

If you're not quite sure what your gift is or what the best way to use it is, that's okay! Ask God. Because if there's anything he loves more than giving good gifts to his kids, it's showing them how to use them.

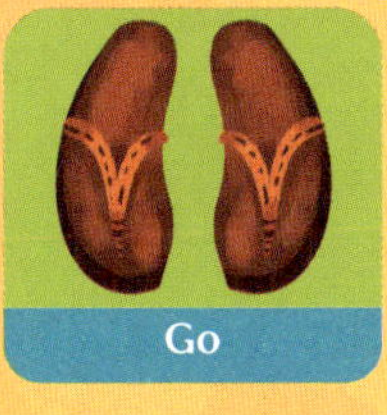

Read All About It

Read more about Samson and his selfishness in Judges 14. (And you can read about that not-so-great ending for Samson in Judges 16.)

Talk About It

Some gifts and talents seem to sparkle a little bit more than others. But everyone's gifts and talents are from God. So is anyone's gift really better than anyone else's? How can we as a family celebrate each other and the things God has made us good at?

Pray About It

God, please help us to see the gifts that you've given us. Teach us to use them to help others and to show the world how good you are. Amen.

Let's Do This

Everyone has a gift, something they're really good at. Take turns telling each person in your family what you believe their gifts are. Include talents (like playing sports or music), but also include spiritual gifts like giving, serving, teaching, hospitality, encouraging, and praying for others. Write them down so you can remember them!

Go Bigger

Remember that list of gifts and talents you made? Pick one talent from each person's list, and make a plan to use all those gifts and talents together. For example, if one person is good at singing, another at hospitality, and another at teaching, you could join together and invite some friends over for snacks, sing praise songs, and put on a puppet show of a Bible story.

23

All Part of the Plan

> We know that God causes everything to work together for the good of those who love God and are called according to his purpose for them.
>
> ROMANS 8:28

Ruth was a foreigner in the land of the Israelites. Naomi's husband had already died when Ruth married Naomi's son in Ruth's homeland of Moab. But ten years later, when Ruth's husband died, the two women returned to Bethlehem in Israel.

They had no money and no way to earn any. To find food, Ruth went out into the fields every day to search for bits of grain dropped by the harvesters.

And that's where the story gets good.

Because, out of all the fields in Bethlehem, Ruth *just so happened* to choose Boaz's field. And Boaz *just so happened* to be not only Naomi's relative, but also a *family redeemer*. That meant he could rescue Ruth and Naomi by marrying Ruth, which is exactly what Boaz did.

Some people would call all those things coincidences. A coincidence is when two or more things happen at the same time by accident. The thing is, God doesn't do coincidences. And nothing he does is by accident.

God had great plans for Ruth and Boaz right from the start. Plans that included them being the great-grandparents of King David and the great-great-whole-lotta-great-grandparents of Jesus. God's plans were kicked into motion when Ruth headed out to that field to gather grain.

God is so amazing that he will use even our everyday, ordinary choices as part of his great plan. We can trust him with all the details of our lives—from the biggest to the smallest. So the

next time you see a "coincidence" in your life, be on the lookout for how it could be part of God's plan.

Read All About It

Read more about Naomi, Ruth, and Boaz in the book of Ruth.

Talk About It

Some people would rather believe in coincidences—that things just happen by accident—than believe in the God who works in our lives. Why do you think that is?

Pray About It

Father God, we know that you have a good and wonderful plan for us and that you use everything in our lives as part of that plan. Thank you for taking such good care of us. Amen.

Let's Do This

Whenever you see something that appears to be a coincidence, remember that there are no coincidences in God's great plans for you or for this world. Shout out (or at least shout out in your heart), "God did that!"

Go Bigger

Find a simple bread recipe and bake it together. Talk about how Ruth gathered grain, separated it from the chaff, and ground it into flour—all before baking it into bread to eat. When your bread is ready, serve it with praise for the God who sometimes uses "coincidences" to make a way to take care of us.

24

Absolutely Anything!

What do you pray about? Help with a big test or healing for a sick friend? It's wonderful to pray about those things. But did you know you can ask God for anything? Even things that seem impossible?

Just like Hannah did.

Hannah lived long ago, in Old Testament times, and she was heartbroken. She had wanted a baby for so long. Her husband's second wife, Peninnah, had children, but Hannah didn't. (And yes, that whole second wife thing is a little weird and not God's original design, but they did things like that back in Old Testament times.) Peninnah was cruel and made fun of Hannah.

One day, the whole family traveled to the Tabernacle for worship. Hannah slipped away to talk to God alone. She poured out her heart to him and wept bitterly as she prayed for a child of her own. Her prayers were so desperate that, even though her lips moved, no sound came out.

Eli the priest spotted her. He thought she was drunk and started to scold her. But when Hannah explained, Eli said, "May the God of Israel grant the request you have asked of him" (1 Samuel 1:17).

God did! The next year, Hannah had a son of her very own. She named him Samuel.

God wants you to tell him your hopes and hurts and impossible dreams—just like Hannah did. Sometimes he'll give you exactly what you asked for. Other times, God will do something different in your life. Either way, you can trust him to respond with the very best answer for you.

Read All About It

Read more about how God answered Hannah's prayer in 1 Samuel 1.

Talk About It

You can talk to God anytime, anywhere, and about absolutely anything. It doesn't have to be at church or bedtime, with your eyes closed and your hands folded. You don't even have to ask for anything—you can just chat with God! Brainstorm all the different places and ways you can pray, along with some things you can talk to him about.

Pray About It

Father God, we are so grateful that you invite us to talk to you—anytime, anywhere, and about anything. We trust you to always answer us in the way that is best for us. Amen.

Let's Do This

Use the Five-Finger Prayer to help you pray. Touch each finger to remind you of different things to pray for:

- Thumb: those closest to you
- Pointer finger: those who point you in the right direction, like teachers, coaches, and pastors
- Tallest finger: your leaders
- Ring finger: the weak, the sick, and the homeless
- Pinkie: the things you need and want for yourself

Go Bigger

Create a special prayer place for you to be alone with God. It could be in a corner of your room, in a closet, or up in a tree outside. Add a Bible, journal, pens and pencils, and comfy pillows if you like. But all you really need is a quiet space and a heart that's ready to talk—and listen!—to God.

25

Every Step of the Way

You're up! It's your turn to jump off the high dive, lead the prayer, give that speech in class, do something big and brave. Will you go for it? Will you give it a try? Or . . . will you run away and hide?

When it was Saul's turn to do something big and brave, he didn't go for it. He didn't give it a try. Nope. Saul ran away and hid!

It happened right after he was chosen to be Israel's first king. God had already sent the prophet Samuel to meet with Saul and anoint him as king. Which means Samuel poured special oil over Saul's head as a sign that he had been chosen by God. (It sounds messy—and it probably was—but it was a really important sign for the ancient Israelites.)

Then it was time for Saul to go public and let everyone know he was their new king. That's when he panicked and forgot who had made him king . . . God. And that's also when Saul went and hid behind a big stack of baggage.

All this hiding happened because Saul forgot that God was with him.

When it's your turn to step up, you might be a little scared—that's okay! Just remember, God is there to help you every step of the way. You can trust him to help you be brave.

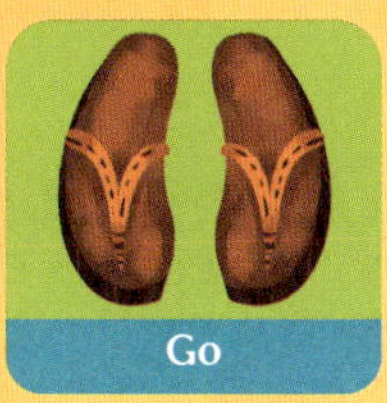

Read All About It

Read more about how Saul became king in 1 Samuel 10.

Talk About It

Being brave doesn't mean you aren't scared. It just means that you trust God to help you face your fears. Take turns sharing times when you were brave or times you know you need to be brave. (Bonus points if it's being brave for God!) Did you remember to pray first? Why is that so important?

Pray About It

Lord, there are times when we are afraid, and we know we need to be brave. Please help us to remember that you are right there with us and that you'll help us face our fears. Amen.

Let's Do This

Challenge yourself today. Do something big and bold and brave. Or not so big or bold, but still brave. (Because little things can be hard sometimes too, right?) Try something new, like a new food or a new friendship. Or invite someone to church. Whatever it is, do something brave. And before you do, don't forget to pray.

Go Bigger

Plan a family adventure day! Plan to do something you've always wanted to try. Maybe it's a rock-climbing gym (or rock climbing outside). It might be zip-lining or going for a hike. It could be a cornfield maze or a trampoline park. But don't just plan it. Pray over it, pick a day, and do it!

Shine Bright!

It's great to be the star, to make the winning shot, to ace the test. Everyone loves being the best, right? But what if your friend gets that number one spot? What do you do when it's their turn to shine?

Do what Jonathan did.

Who is Jonathan? you ask. Jonathan was King Saul's son. He was the prince. And he should have been Israel's next king. Except . . . God chose David, Jonathan's best friend, instead.

Jonathan could have thrown a fit. He could have refused to ever speak to David again. He could have even started a war! But Jonathan didn't do any of those things. He chose to help David shine. Not just once or twice. But every chance he got. Jonathan even saved David's life.

Was it easy? Probably not. Would it have been cool to be king? Probably so. But Jonathan knew God had chosen David. And he loved God and his friend more than he loved himself.

So, the next time a friend comes in first even though you're not far behind . . . or if they get chosen and you do not . . . or if they get that thing you wanted for yourself, remember this: In God's eyes, you shine brightest when you help someone else shine.

Read All About It

Read more about Jonathan's amazing friendship with David in 1 Samuel 20.

Talk About It

Think about the friends in your life. What are the things you love about them? What makes a great friend . . . and what makes a not-so-great friend? How can you be a better friend?

Pray About It

Father God, friendship is a gift you give to us, and it's a gift we can give to each other. Help us think of others first and be the best friends we can be. Amen.

Let's Do This

It is often said that the way to have good friends is to *be* a good friend. Do something a little extra special for a friend today. It could be an encouraging text, a shared treat, or just extra time hanging out with them.

Go Bigger

To remind yourself of how wonderful friendship is, make friendship bracelets for yourself and your friends. Ask a grown-up to help you find instructions and gather supplies. Then sit down and create! (Bonus points if you invite your friends over and make them together.)

Always Moving

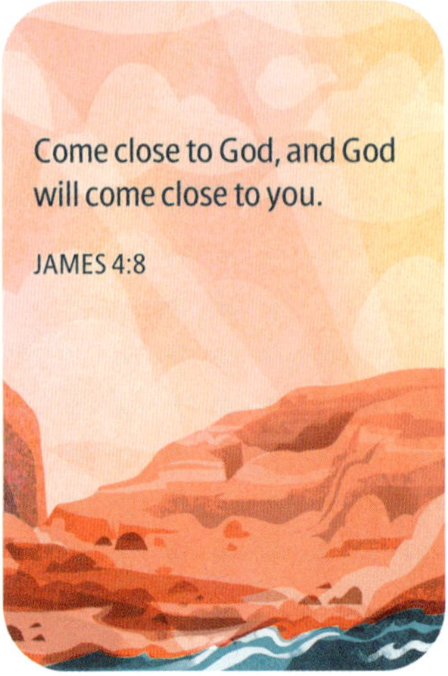

Don't move! Not a millimeter. Stand *completely* still. Can you do it? It's practically impossible! Sooner or later, you'll lean a little, sway to one side, or lose your balance completely. No matter how hard you try, you can't stay completely still for long.

You can't stay completely still in your relationship with God either. You're always moving one way or the other. If you don't focus on moving closer to God, then guess what will happen? You'll move further away.

King Saul discovered that the hard way. He stopped focusing on God and what God wanted. Instead, Saul focused on himself and what *he* wanted.

Like the time Saul was preparing to do battle with Israel's enemies. He was supposed to wait for the prophet Samuel to come and offer a sacrifice to God before the battle. But Saul got tired of waiting and offered the sacrifice himself (see 1 Samuel 13:7-14). Or the time Saul kept his enemy's cattle when God told him not to (see 1 Samuel 15:1-9), or all the many times he tried to kill David so he could keep on being king.

All because Saul stopped focusing on God.

When you don't keep your eyes and your heart focused on God—when you don't obey him and fill your life with his Word—other stuff slips in and pulls you away from him. It could be bad things, or it might be so many good things there isn't room for God. Fill your life with things that please God, and keep moving closer to him.

Read All About It

Read about how far Saul moved away from God in 1 Samuel 13 and 15.

Talk About It

God is always with us. He never leaves us. But sometimes we wander away from doing his will. What are some ways you can make sure you're sticking close to God and always moving toward him?

Pray About It

God, please help us to keep our eyes and our hearts focused on you. If we ever stop moving toward you or start moving away, please pull us back. Amen.

Let's Do This

As you move through your day today—whether it's walking to your room, riding to school, or biking through your backyard—think about God and how good he is. Before you know it, you'll be moving closer to him!

Go Bigger

How long can you stand on one foot? Gather family and/or friends and make it a competition. Who can stand on one foot the longest? Can you stand longer on your right foot or your left? What happens if you keep switching from one foot to the other?

28

What Would You Ask For?

> If you need wisdom, ask our generous God, and he will give it to you. He will not rebuke you for asking.
>
> JAMES 1:5

If you could ask God for anything—anything in the world—what would it be? Piles of money? An end to all homework? To be the greatest scientist, soccer player, or musician of all time?

That's the decision Solomon got to make when he first became king of Israel. God came to him in a dream and said, "What do you want? Ask, and I will give it to you!" (1 Kings 3:5).

Anything? Wow! Solomon could have asked for more power or riches or a long life. But he didn't ask for any of those things. Instead, Solomon asked for wisdom and "an understanding heart" so that he could be a good king for God's people. He wanted to "know the difference between right and wrong" in order to make wise decisions (1 Kings 3:9).

God was so pleased with Solomon's request that he not only gave him wisdom and understanding, but he also gave him the wealth, power, and long life that he didn't ask for.

God's long-ago question wasn't just for Solomon. It's for you too. The fact is, you *can* ask God for anything. Sometimes he'll say yes and bless you with exactly what you asked for. Other times, he'll answer your prayer in a different way. But he'll always answer with what he knows you need.

So whatever situation you're facing in your day today—whether it's something good, something tough, or something that's just kind of tricky to figure out—ask God. Ask him for his wisdom to help you know what to do. It's a prayer God loves to answer!

Read All About It

Read more about Solomon's request in 1 Kings 3:5-14.

Talk About It

Some people treat God like a vending machine. They "drop in" their prayer and expect God to "drop out" the exact thing they asked for. But that's not how God does things. And we shouldn't pray only to get what we want. Discuss how prayer is also about listening, trusting God with our troubles, and building a friendship with him.

Pray About It

Lord, you know the perfect answer for every prayer we pray. Help us trust that your answers are the best answers. Amen.

Let's Do This

Think about it: If you could ask for anything in the world, what would you ask for? Would it be things you need or things you dream about? For yourself? For others? For God? Would your answer make God smile?

Go Bigger

The Bible tells us, "Where two or three gather together as my followers, I am there among them" (Matthew 18:20). Is there a prayer group at your school, in your neighborhood, or at church? Reach out and ask if you can join in! Because God loves when his people pray for each other. (And if you can't find a group, try starting one yourself.)

29

Putting God First

In Bible times, people would sometimes worship idols, or statues, made of wood, metal, or stone. These false gods couldn't speak or move or really do anything at all. Not only were these idols powerless to help people, but they actually hurt them by pulling them away from God.

To protect his people from idols, God gave Israel very specific instructions for how to worship him—and *only* him. King Jeroboam didn't obey God's instructions. Instead, he set up two golden calves and actually led the people in worshiping them!

Now, you probably aren't planning on bowing down to a couple of golden cows any time soon. But you still need to keep an eye out for idols.

That's because today's idols are sneakier and harder to spot. It's easy for us to look at a statue and wonder why the Israelites would be tempted to worship it. After all, it's just a hunk of wood or metal or stone. It can't *do* anything.

But not all idols are statues, and not all idols are made of wood, metal, or stone. In today's world, an idol is more likely to be something like power or money. Idols can even be good things like sports, grades, or friends. That's because an idol is anything we let become more important than God. When we "worship" something by giving it all our time and attention—that's when good things can go bad.

Is there an idol in your life? Is something stealing your attention away from God? Ask God to help you put that thing back in its place and put him first!

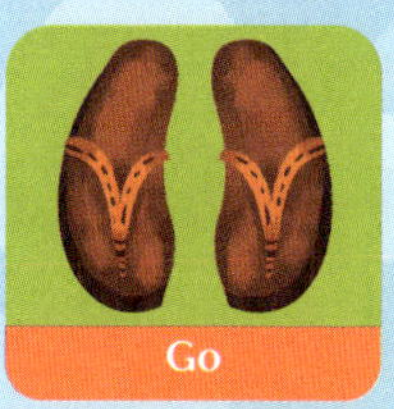

Read All About It

Read more about King Jeroboam's idols in 1 Kings 12:25-30.

Talk About It

Idols can slip in and take over before we realize it. They eat up our time and money and energy. What are some of the idols we see people struggling with today? Do we struggle with any ourselves? Why is it so hard to say no to them?

Pray About It

Lord, please show us anything that is coming between us and you. We want to worship you—and only you—with our time, our money, and our hearts. Amen.

Let's Do This

True worship is about loving God and loving others (see Matthew 22:37-39). Challenge yourself today to do something that shows you love God, such as sing a praise song or tell someone about him. And challenge yourself to do something that shows you love your neighbor.

Go Bigger

As a family, create a chart of your family's time throughout the week. Block out the things you *have* to do like work, go to school, and sleep. But take a closer look at your free time. How much of that time is about you and what you want? How much is about God and others? Do you need to make some changes?

You're Never Alone

"Don't be afraid!" Elisha told him. "For there are more on our side than on theirs!"

2 KINGS 6:16

Have you ever felt surrounded by worries, troubles, or even enemies?

In Old Testament times, Elisha the prophet and his servant certainly felt that way. Probably because they really were surrounded!

Elisha's enemy, the king of Aram, was so furious with him that he sent his huge army of troops, chariots, and horses to surround the city where Elisha and his servant were staying. When the servant got up the next morning and saw all those horses, troops, and chariots everywhere, he was terrified. But Elisha wasn't. He knew something the servant didn't know. He knew they weren't alone.

"Don't be afraid!" Elisha told him. "For there are more on our side than on theirs!" Then Elisha prayed for God to open the servant's eyes "and let him see!" (2 Kings 6:16-17). The servant looked again, and this time he saw that the hills around them were filled with an army with chariots of fire. It was the Lord's angel army!

There will be times when you feel surrounded by worries, troubles, and even enemies. You might think, *It's going to take a battle to get out of this!* When that happens, just remember: you're not facing that battle alone. You—and all those worries and troubles—are surrounded by God and his angel army.

God is bigger and stronger than any worry, trouble, or enemy could ever be. And he will fight for you. (Spoiler alert: God wins. Every single time!)

Read All About It

Read more about God and his invisible army in 2 Kings 6:8-23.

Talk About It

God is always working in our lives. Sometimes we see it, but other times we don't. How does this story of Elijah and his servant help you remember that God is working even when we don't see him?

Pray About It

Lord, thank you for watching over us and protecting us—in all the ways we see and all the ways we don't see. Amen.

Let's Do This

Help yourself remember that you never face any trouble alone by memorizing God's promises. Like this one from Isaiah 41:10: "Don't be afraid, for I am with you." Repeat this promise whenever you feel surrounded by trouble.

Go Bigger

Draw a picture of God's invisible army on a piece of heavy white paper using a white crayon. Can you see it? No! Now, use a brush to paint your page with watercolor paint—and reveal the angel army!

31

When You've Made a Mess

> If we confess our sins to him, he is faithful and just to forgive us our sins and to cleanse us from all wickedness.
>
> 1 JOHN 1:9

Have you ever made a mess? Spilled the cereal, tracked in mud, had a silly argument with a friend? Or maybe you knew the right thing to do—the thing God wanted you to do—and made a mess by choosing to do wrong instead.

That's exactly what God's people did in the time of Israel's kings. Not spilled the cereal or tracked in mud. No, they did something far worse than that. They knew what God wanted them to do. They knew what was right and what was wrong. And they chose to do wrong so many times.

Because they chose wrong, there were consequences. *Terrible ones!* Enemies attacked, the Temple was destroyed, and many of God's people were taken as captives to Babylon.

Even after all the wrong things the people had done, even with the Temple destroyed and the people taken away, God still loved them and wanted the best for them. So he waited for them to turn back to him. He waited for them to turn away from their sins. And when they did, he was ready to rescue them again.

You can always sweep up the cereal, wipe up the mud, or apologize to your friend. But what happens if the mess you've made is bigger? What happens if the mess you've made is with God?

Tell God you're sorry. Ask him to forgive you. Because he's just waiting to rescue you, forgive you, and say, *Welcome back! I've really missed you!*

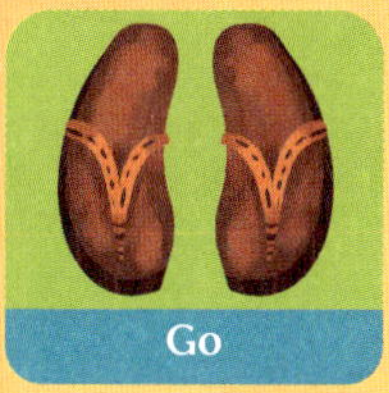

Read All About It

Read more about the mess God's people made in 2 Kings 25.

Talk About It

If we mess up and sin, God promises to forgive us when we confess what we've done (see 1 John 1:9). To *confess* is more than just telling God what we did. It's agreeing with him that what we did was wrong. No excuses. No trying to explain. Just confessing. Why is it important to admit we were wrong? Why is that sometimes so hard to do?

Pray About It

God, help us to see the wrong things that we do. And then help us to hurry to confess them to you. Amen.

Let's Do This

If you realize you've done something wrong, don't ignore it. Don't wait to ask God to forgive you. Ask right away!

Go Bigger

Fill a backpack with heavy books or cans. Then put it on and try to walk across the room. Not easy, is it? Empty the backpack and take that walk again. Much easier, right? That heavy backpack is like sin. It weighs us down and makes it harder to follow God. But when we confess and ask God to take away our sins, he removes that heavy burden—and makes it much easier to follow him.

All Together

The body has many different parts, not just one part.

1 CORINTHIANS 12:14

When the Israelites at last returned to the Promised Land from their captivity in Babylon, they needed to do a lot of rebuilding. The city of Jerusalem was in terrible shape, the Temple was in ruins, and parts of the city wall were completely torn down. Builders were very needed in those days!

But not everyone was a builder. Did the other people matter? Were they needed too? Of course! All the people were needed. Priests helped the people worship. Bakers kept everyone fed. Musicians cheered up the builders and lightened the workload with their songs. And guards kept everyone safe from the enemies who still roamed the land.

Every single person was needed. And they all worked together, using the gifts and talents God had given them.

Every single person is needed in our churches today too. Think about it. If there were only pastors and speakers, who would sing? If there were only singers, who would teach? And if there were no one to clean up or put things away, what a mess there would be!

God gives each and every person a talent—and that includes you! You can do things no one else can do in quite the same way as you. That means you are needed—in God's church, God's world, and God's Kingdom. (Hint: That means everyone else is needed too.)

When you add your gifts and talents to everyone else's, church truly becomes a heavenly place to be!

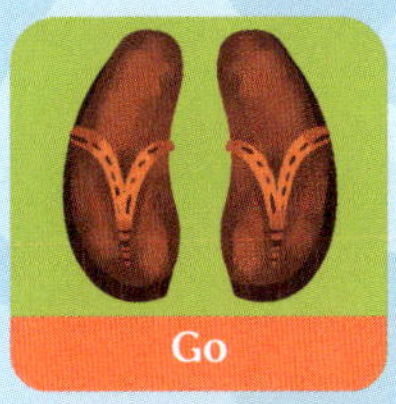

Read All About It

Read more about the rebuilding of Jerusalem in 1 Chronicles 9:22-34 and Nehemiah 1–3.

Talk About It

People do lots of different kinds of things around a church. There are the people everyone sees up front, like the pastor or song leader. There are the people only a few see, like Sunday school teachers and office workers. Then there are the people very few see, like the employees or volunteers who clean the buildings and mow the grass. How is each person important and needed?

Pray About It

Lord, thank you for the gifts and talents you've given each one of us. Help us see all the opportunities you give us to use them. Amen.

Let's Do This

Think of something you're especially good at. It might be singing, sports, drawing, praying, or encouraging others. Use your talent to make someone smile today.

Go Bigger

Tap into the whole family's talents to host a yard sale. Put each person in charge of one part of the project, such as gathering stuff to sell, making signs, counting out change, and talking to customers. When the sale is done, donate the profits to a project at church—the way the Israelites donated money to help rebuild their Temple (see Ezra 1:6).

Don't Hesitate

The LORD is compassionate and merciful, slow to get angry and filled with unfailing love.

PSALM 103:8

When we do what's right, our actions are a good example for others. But what about when we mess up and sin? Can we still be a good example? Yes! When we turn back to God without hesitating.

King Hezekiah showed how to do that. You see, Jerusalem was the capital city of God's people. It should have been a shining example of how to love and worship God. But it wasn't.

For years, Hezekiah's father—the evil King Ahaz—worshiped false gods. He gave some of the Temple's treasures to foreign kings, moved the altar, and broke up some of the furniture used in the Temple. Then he shut the Temple doors and built altars all around the land so that the people could worship those fake gods!

Then Hezekiah became king.

Hezekiah knew the people were doing wrong. In his first month as king, he ordered the priests to reopen the Temple and destroy the idols and altars to fake gods. Then he led the people in worshiping the one true God. They sang and shared a Passover feast.

Hezekiah showed the people how to turn back to God—and he shows us the same thing today.

We all mess up and sin. If people see our bad examples, let's also show them a good example of turning back to God. Let's show them how we tell God we're sorry, how we praise him for forgiving us, and how we try to do right.

Because what we do *after* we mess up lets others know that they can turn back to God too.

Read All About It

Read more about King Hezekiah's good example in 2 Chronicles 29–30.

Talk About It

When was the last time you did something wrong? Maybe you were upset and acted out in anger. Or maybe you got caught up in a conversation that slipped into gossip. It happens! What matters is what you do next. Share some ways you can be a good example *after* you've messed up.

Pray About It

Father God, we confess that sometimes we sin. When that happens, help us to show the world what it looks like to turn back to you. Amen.

Let's Do This

The second you realize that your attitude—and maybe your actions too—are not what they should be, stop. Drop to your knees—either in real life or in your heart. Tell God you're sorry. Apologize to anyone else you've hurt. Don't hesitate to make it right.

Go Bigger

Remember that conversation you had in "Talk About It"? Act it out. Role-play how to be a good example when you lose your cool, when you gossip in a conversation, or any of the other situations you thought of.

34

Don't Let It Stop You

Don't repay evil for evil. Don't retaliate with insults when people insult you. Instead, pay them back with a blessing.

1 PETER 3:9

Have you ever met someone who wanted you to mess up? Maybe they made fun of you, tripped you in gym class, or tried to stop you from doing what you needed to do. What do you do when others are mean?

Nehemiah knew a thing or two about people like that. When he returned to Jerusalem from captivity, he discovered that the city wall was in terrible shape. This was the wall that protected the people from their enemies. In some places, there were huge holes, and in other places, parts of the wall were completely missing.

Nehemiah knew they desperately needed to get their wall fixed—and fast. He gathered the Israelites and told them his plan to rebuild. He even had the king's permission and help. The people were excited and ready to get to work. Except for three men—Sanballat, Tobiah, and Geshem. They didn't like it one bit! (They also didn't live there. They were enemies of the Jewish people and wanted the wall to stay open to attack.)

Sanballat, Tobiah, and Geshem laughed and scoffed and threatened. They even accused Nehemiah of rebelling against the king. They wanted to make the people afraid so they would stop working on the wall.

But check out what Nehemiah said: "The God of heaven will help us succeed" (Nehemiah 2:20). And that's exactly what God did. The wall was rebuilt in record time!

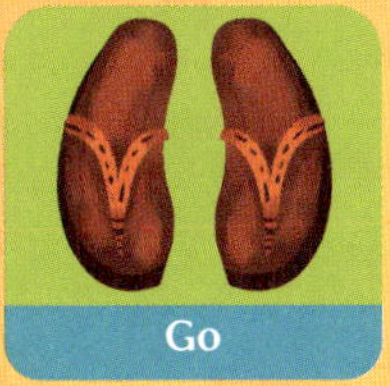

When people are mean, don't try to hurt them back. Be kind instead. Pray for them, pray for wisdom, and trust God to help you succeed.

Read All About It

Read more about Nehemiah and his plan to rebuild Jerusalem's wall in Nehemiah 2.

Talk About It

It's hard to understand why some people are rude, full of hate and anger, or just plain mean. Maybe they're having a really rotten day, their parents are fighting, or they feel sick. Or perhaps they just don't want you to succeed. Knowing the reason doesn't make it right, but could it help you understand and forgive? Could it help you know how to pray for them?

Pray About It

Lord, when people are hurtful or unkind or just plain mean, remind us to bring our hurts to you. Please give us the strength not to be mean back to them. Amen.

Let's Do This

You know that person who kind of gets on your nerves? Maybe they're even a little mean sometimes . . . or a lot of times. Look for something kind you can do for them. (And if that doesn't feel safe, pray for them.)

Go Bigger

Nehemiah used stones to rebuild Jerusalem's wall—stones that didn't fall down! Work together with family and friends to build your own "wall" by creating a domino toppling train that *will* fall down. Stand the dominoes on end just a little space apart. Create a wall in the shape of a circle or a line. Take turns starting the toppling train.

A Time to Be Brave

Even when I walk through the darkest valley, I will not be afraid, for you are close beside me. Your rod and your staff protect and comfort me.

PSALM 23:4

You were born in this time and place for a reason. God has a plan for you, and he's getting you ready for all that he wants you to do.

The question is, Will you be brave and live out God's plan for you?

That's the question Queen Esther faced long ago. An evil man named Haman was plotting to have all the Jews killed, and he tricked the king into agreeing. When Esther's cousin Mordecai found out, he sent a message begging her to go to the king and save her people.

There were two problems with that. First, no one in the royal court knew that Esther was Jewish, not even the king. And second, if Esther went to the king uninvited, she could be killed too!

Esther was frightened. She didn't think she could do it. She wasn't sure she was brave enough to try. But Mordecai said, "Who knows if perhaps you were made queen for just such a time as this?" (Esther 4:14).

Esther decided to be brave, but not on her own. She fasted and prayed for three days. Then she went to see the king . . . and her people were saved.

All because Esther turned to God to help her be brave.

There will be a time when God asks you to be brave. It might be standing up for others, telling the truth when it would be easier to lie, or doing right when everyone else is choosing wrong. Whatever God asks you to do, know that he'll be right there helping you be brave.

Read All About It

Read more about Esther's courage in Esther 4.

Talk About It

Being brave doesn't mean that you aren't still a little scared. And being a little (or a lot) scared doesn't mean you aren't brave. When do you need to be brave? Is there something you need to do that scares you? How can you ask God to help you be brave?

Pray About It

God, when we are scared, we know you will help us to be brave. Thank you for never leaving us to face anything on our own. Amen.

Let's Do This

Challenge yourself to do something a little brave today. Try something new, invite a friend to church, or offer to pray with someone. What brave thing can you do?

Go Bigger

Gather as a family and give each person time to share something that is hard for them—that even scares them. Discuss ways you can encourage each other and help each other to be brave.

36

When Bad Things Happen

> When troubles of any kind come your way, consider it an opportunity for great joy. For you know that when your faith is tested, your endurance has a chance to grow.
>
> JAMES 1:2-3

Why do bad things happen to us and the people we love?

That's the question Job was asking. You see, Job loved God with all his heart. He always tried to do what was good and right, and God blessed him for that. But Satan wanted to test Job. He wanted to see if Job really loved God, or if he just loved the things God had given him.

God gave Satan permission to test Job. So, one by one, Satan took away Job's gifts from God. He took Job's family, his flocks and herds of animals, his servants, and his health. Job couldn't understand why all these terrible things were happening. He even asked God why.

The thing is, we humans can't understand the ways God works or thinks (see Isaiah 55:8-9). But God did listen to Job. And when Job refused to turn away from God, he blessed Job even more than before.

Maybe you tried to do everything right, but it still went all wrong. Or the best person you know is hurting. Or a terrible storm came and destroyed your home or your school. Bad things do happen to good people in our world because of *sin*. It came into God's perfect world all the way back in the garden of Eden when Adam and Eve chose to disobey God, and it messed up *everything*.

While our world isn't perfect anymore, God is. Life might get rough sometimes, but God will always keep his promise to take care of us. Our job is to keep trusting him, and one day Jesus will return and transform the earth into a place where only good things happen.

Read All About It

Read more about Job's troubles in Job 1–2.

Talk About It

Sin doesn't just affect the person who chooses wrong. It affects the people around them too. For example, if someone tells a lie about another person, that lie touches those who listen to it, believe it, and pass it on, as well as the one being lied about. How can this cause bad things to happen to people who haven't done anything wrong?

Pray About It

God, when troubles come our way, we usually think they are all bad. Help us to see them as a chance to learn to trust you even more. Amen.

Let's Do This

When you see something bad happening to someone else—whether it's a big thing or a little thing that feels big—don't just stand by and watch. Do something to brighten their dark day. It could be a hug, a helping hand, or simply sitting with them.

Go Bigger

Be the good when bad happens. Prepare an emergency kit for disasters like storms or floods, or even for simply when the power goes out. Pack your kit with items such as water bottles, flashlights and batteries, bandages, and other emergency supplies. Make one for your family and one to share with a friend.

God Made It All

God created everything in the heavenly realms and on earth. He made the things we can see and the things we can't see.

COLOSSIANS 1:16

Some people say this world just *happened.* That it was all one big cosmic accident. But they're wrong. This world and everything in it—from the tallest mountain to the deepest sea and everything in between—was handcrafted by God. Every single detail was planned by him. He designed all those details to work together to make this world, this universe, and everything in it, well, *work.*

For example, sunlight helps the plants and flowers grow, which give the animals food to eat. Fish swim in oceans whose waves are controlled by the moon. Birds nest in trees that grew tall from tiny seeds. God made all these things!

The more we study God's creation, the more we discover. There are still places on the earth and deep beneath the sea that no one has ever seen. And then there's the vastness of space still to explore! There's no end to the discoveries we can make in God's creation because there's no end to God.

But stars and oceans and animals aren't the only things handcrafted by God. *You* are handcrafted by God too. In fact, you're his masterpiece. Because in all the vastness of this earth and the universe beyond, only people are created to be like him. Only we are created to do good works in his world (see Ephesians 2:10). And only we can tell the world just how powerful and amazing our Creator God is. Who will you tell?

Read All About It

Read more about God's creation in Job 38–39.

Talk About It

Read through Job 38–39 and notice all the amazing things God has done and continues to do. How many animals can you find? What did God teach them? What do these passages say about the wind and rain and snow? What does that tell you about the power of God?

Pray About It

Lord, you tell the lightning which way to go and the stars how to shine. You can do anything! So we know we can trust you to take care of anything we need. Amen.

Let's Do This

As you walk along today, notice the things God has made—from the sky and clouds to the trees to your friends and family. How many things can you find? Be sure to thank him for each one.

Go Bigger

Grab a magnifying glass and head out for a backyard safari. Look at a blade of grass, a rock, a drop of water, a leaf, and a hand. Do you see all the details in even the most ordinary things? God made those! What other wonders can you find?

Welcome to the Family!

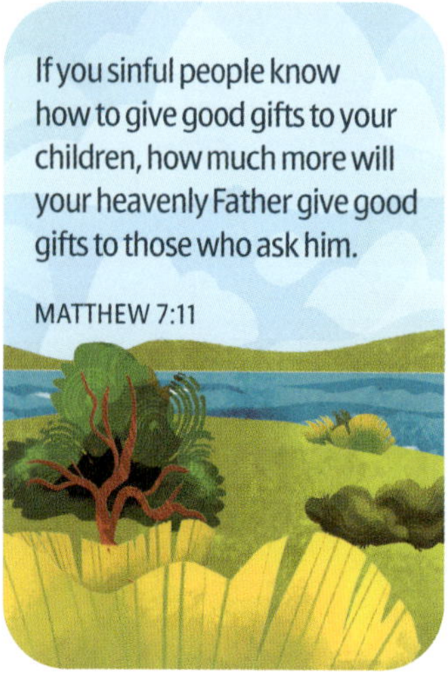

Imagine the perfect family. What would it look like? Everyone's description might be a little different. But there are some things that we would all want in a perfect family. Things like being loved no matter what, feeling safe and wanted, and being taken care of. We'd want a family we could trust and count on and where we would always be welcome.

Some families are wonderful and pretty close to being all of that. Sure, they may disagree or argue once in a while, but they love and help each other too. Other families aren't so great. They don't love or help each other like they should. And even in the best families, people make mistakes—the grown-ups and the kids.

Because no one is perfect, that means no family is perfect either. At least no family here on earth. But God's family? That's a different story.

God is the perfect dad. With him, you're always loved, safe, wanted, and taken care of. You can trust him and count on him. Forever and always. No matter what.

In your human family, there may be times when you hurt each other's feelings or get upset with each other. When that happens, you might feel sad and on your own.

But you don't ever have to be alone. No matter what your family here on earth is like, God wants to adopt you into *his* family. When you decide to believe in and follow his Son, Jesus, he opens his arms up wide and says . . . *Welcome home!*

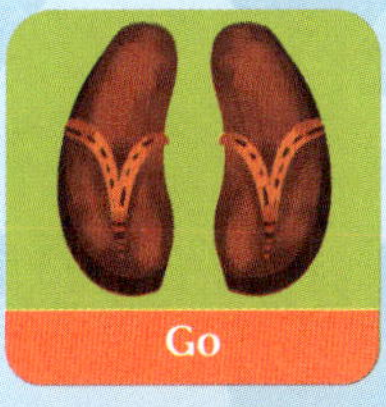

Read All About It

Read more about God's family in Psalm 68:5-6.

Talk About It

Imagine the perfect family. What would it be like? How would the family members treat each other? What would they do if someone made a mistake or chose to do wrong? What does it mean that God is the perfect parent?

Pray About It

Father God, you are perfect in every way. Thank you for inviting us to be part of your family. Help us to love each other the way you love us. Amen.

Let's Do This

Who taught you about God? Say a prayer thanking God for them, and then ask God to show you who you can tell about him.

Go Bigger

What are the stories of your family's faith? Interview your parents, grandparents, or other family members who have helped you learn about God. Ask them questions like *When did you first believe? Who told you about God?* and *When was a time God helped you through something hard?* Take pictures and/or record them on video, if you can. Use the pictures and stories to create a family faith book.

39

The Most Amazing Stories

Give thanks to the LORD and proclaim his greatness. Let the whole world know what he has done.

PSALM 105:1

Did you know little kids are looking up to you? That's right! Because in their eyes, you're the big kid—the cool kid—and they're eager to listen to you. Especially when you tell them stories. So which stories are you going to tell them?

Will you tell them about a snowy world on the other side of a wardrobe, where animals talk and a lion named Aslan rules the land? Maybe you'll tell them stories of glass slippers, adventurous rabbits who are always running late, or a beast who would like to be a prince again. Or you could spin a story filled with pirates, crocodiles, adventure, and saving the day.

Those are all wonderful stories to tell—and you should definitely find a time to share them. But don't forget to tell the greatest story of all to those kids looking up to you and listening to you.

Tell them the true story of God, how he created each of them, and how much he loves them. You're not too young—you're never too young—to start spreading God's Word. So read stories from the Bible to younger kids, or help them act out these stories in a puppet show. And be sure to tell them about the times God has helped you.

Sharing your faith and these stories of God will not only bless those little ones, but it will also bless you as you remember how great and wonderful God is.

Read All About It

Read more about sharing stories of God in Psalm 78:1-4.

Talk About It

Before people had the written Bible, they shared about God and his great big love with stories spoken aloud. Jesus himself often told stories called parables to teach the people. What makes stories such a wonderful way to tell others about God? What are your favorite stories about God?

Pray About It

God, there are still so many people who need to hear about you. Please lead us to the people you want us to talk to—and then help us to be bold enough to tell your story. Amen.

Let's Do This

The Bible is packed with true stories of all kinds. Choose your favorite story from the Bible and draw it out in pictures. Then use the drawings like a picture book to share the story with someone younger than you.

Go Bigger

Have a family story night. Gather up robes, belts, sashes, and crowns—and any other costume pieces you have. Dress up and pretend you're a storyteller from long ago. Take turns telling your favorite stories from the Bible. Be sure to add lots of drama and even sound effects!

You Are Made to Create!

The heavens proclaim the glory of God. The skies display his craftsmanship.

PSALM 19:1

God didn't have to do it, you know. He didn't have to make stars that twinkle or sunrises that streak across the sky in more colors than the rainbow. He didn't have to give giraffes those extra-long necks or paint the mask on the racoon. The mountains didn't have to soar, and lions would still be lions even without their mighty roars.

No, God didn't have to do all those things. But he did . . . and so much more! God was the one who chose the colors for each butterfly's wings. He painted the flowers and shaped their leaves. It was God who taught the birds to chirp their melodies and gave the ocean waves their rhythm. There's no end to the wonder and creativity of God. It's everywhere and all around you!

But here's something you might not know. Because you are made in God's image, his creativity is in you . . . making you creative too!

You might be a painter, a writer, or a singer of songs. Maybe you're a whiz at solving problems, fixing machines, or inventing things. Or perhaps you find the most wonderful ways to encourage, help, and serve.

Whatever shape your creativity takes, God gave it to you for a reason. He wants you to use it to show the world—or at least your little corner of it—about him and how huge his love for them is. So . . . what will you create today?

Read All About It

Read more about God's creativity in Psalm 104.

Talk About It

Have one person read Psalm 104 aloud while everyone else closes their eyes and opens up their imaginations. Let the words paint a picture in your mind. Take turns sharing what was most amazing to each of you.

Pray About It

Lord, no one else could ever create the things you've made. Thank you for filling this world with wonders that remind us of you. Amen.

Let's Do This

Creativity needs a little time and quiet to happen. So try some daydreaming today. (Not in class or when you're supposed to be doing homework!) Let your mind wander while you ask God to fill your mind with ideas to create.

Go Bigger

As a family, plan a creativity garden. It can be outdoors in the ground or indoors in pots. Let each person use their creative skills to help. Artists can pick colors and plant flowers. Organizers can decide where each plant goes, while the math whiz might keep track of the seeds. Let everyone's creativity shine!

No One Like You

Thank you for making me so wonderfully complex! Your workmanship is marvelous—how well I know it.

PSALM 139:14

There's no one like you. You are wonderful, amazing, and marvelous—because that's how God made you. He created you to do things no one else can do quite like you. He made you so marvelous that you'll be discovering those things your whole life through.

The evil in this world, though—it doesn't want you to know how special you are. It wants you to think you're just one more person in a crowded world. But there's something you need to remember: The evil in this world lies (John 8:44). Here's the truth: Not only are you wonderfully made by God, but when you choose to follow him, you are also

- chosen, royal, holy, and God's own special possession (1 Peter 2:9);
- a masterpiece (Ephesians 2:10) made by the God who has such good plans for you (Jeremiah 29:11);
- his child and an heir with Christ (Romans 8:16-17);
- endlessly loved (1 John 3:1); and
- so loved that God sent his own Son to save you (John 3:16).

Believe these truths. Tell them to anyone and everyone who'll listen. Go out into this world . . . and be wonderful, amazing, marvelous you!

Read All About It

Read more about how wonderfully God made you in Psalm 139.

Talk About It

Talk about your earliest memories of each other. Parents and grandparents, share your memories of the first time you met your child or grandchild. And kids? Share about the first thing you can remember about each person.

Pray About It

God, sometimes it's so easy to see all the things about ourselves we wish we could change. Help us, instead, to see how wonderful you made us. Amen.

Let's Do This

Look in the mirror and smile at the person you see. Then say to yourself, "God made me, and his work is marvelous!"

Go Bigger

Pull out the family pictures and talk about where each person got their looks and habits from. Do you have your grandpa's red hair or your grandma's smile? Do you have your dad's nose, your mom's eyes, or your aunt's giggle? If you're adopted, you might not *look* like each other, but maybe you tell jokes like your dad, paint like your mom, or love helping others like your grandpa. Next, share about the things each of you got from God, like your joyful heart, encouraging spirit, kindness, and love.

42

Choosing Wisely

Walk with the wise and become wise; associate with fools and get in trouble.

PROVERBS 13:20

Have you ever been hanging out with someone and realized you're starting to act like them? You say the same words at the same time and giggle at the same jokes. And that feels kind of great, doesn't it?

But what happens if those words turn into ones you know you shouldn't say? Or the jokes are making fun of someone else?

Proverbs 13:20 says you become more and more like the people you hang out with, so you need to choose those people wisely.

Friendships are so important in your life. You *need* friends. But you'll find that there are different kinds of friendships. Some will be friends you hang out with in certain places, like in classes you share or at practices. They're fun to talk to. You might study together, eat lunch together, or just hang out sometimes. You still need to be careful and make sure they're not tempting you to make bad choices. But mostly you're just sharing your time with them. You might have lots of friends like this.

Best friends are different. You might only have one or two of them. You hang out together, laugh, and have fun. But these are the friends you'll also share your heart with. So you need to be extra careful when choosing them. Best friends love God, pray for each other, cheer each other on, and love each other enough to say something if the other person is doing wrong. Ask God to bring that kind of best friend into your life—and to help you be that kind of best friend too.

Read All About It

Read more about making wise choices and what to look for in a friend in Proverbs 13.

Talk About It

Friendships are so important. We need others we can laugh with, spend time with, and count on to help us. We especially need friends who will help us stick close to God. Philippians 2:3 is a great guide for how to be a good friend. Read it out loud and share ways you can be this kind of friend.

Pray About It

Lord, thank you for the gift of friendship. Show us how to choose good friends who will help us stick close to you. And guide us to be that kind of friend for others. Amen.

Let's Do This

John 15:15 says that when you decide to follow Jesus, he calls you *his* friend. Spend a few minutes today just thinking about how awesome it is to be a friend of Jesus.

Go Bigger

Some of the best friendships can be the ones right in your own family. Grab some paper and pencils. Have each person write a note to every other family member. In the note, list one thing you love about that person and one thing you're grateful for. Swap notes, and then dive in for a group hug!

43

Washed Away

"Come now, let's settle this," says the LORD. "Though your sins are like scarlet, I will make them as white as snow."

ISAIAH 1:18

Have you ever gotten a glob of ketchup on your shirt? You tried everything, but you just couldn't wash that stain out.

Sin is kind of like that. It stains our hearts and souls blood red. Every hateful word, every unkind thought, and every lie makes the stain bigger and darker. Nothing *we* do will ever remove that stain.

And that's why Jesus came. God knows we can never completely stop sinning on our own, no matter how hard we try. (Have you ever tried to go a whole day without doing or saying or thinking one single thing wrong? Without making any mistakes? You might get close, but some sin always sneaks in.) God also knew we could never get rid of the stains of sin. We can't save ourselves, and we can't make our own way to God. So he sent his Son, Jesus.

Jesus came to earth and lived a perfect life. And even though he never once sinned, he died on the cross to take the punishment for all our sins. His death made it possible for our sins to be washed away. When Jesus rose up out of the grave, he made a way for us be with God forever.

When you believe in Jesus—when you choose to love and follow him—it's like he makes a trade with you. He takes all the filthy stained "clothes" of your sin and guilt, and he gives you his own snowy-white robes of perfection instead, so that you can be free from sin and part of God's family.

Read All About It

Read more about how God cleanses us from our sins in Isaiah 1:18 and 1 John 1:7-9.

Talk About It

Some things you have to earn, like an allowance, a spot on the team, or a part in the play. But no matter what you do or how hard you try, you can't earn God's grace. Grace is the gift of God's forgiveness, and all we have to do is accept it. Talk about why we can't earn our forgiveness. Why is it sometimes hard to accept a gift, especially one as big as grace?

Pray About It

God, we could never say thank-you enough for your grace. Please help us to live our whole lives showing you how grateful we are. Amen.

Let's Do This

Psalm 139:24 asks God to "point out anything in me that offends you," which means the psalmist is praying that God will show him anything he needs to be forgiven for. Pray this prayer today. Watch and listen for the sins God shows you, and then ask him to forgive you.

Go Bigger

Make your own snowy-white snow! In a big bowl, mix together 1 cup of baking soda with 1 cup of shaving cream (the plain white foamy kind). Use your hands to mix it together until it starts to clump up like snow. (If the mixture is too sticky, add a little more baking soda.) The "snow" will even get cold!

44

The Potter and the Clay

> God, who began the good work within you, will continue his work until it is finally finished on the day when Christ Jesus returns.
>
> PHILIPPIANS 1:6

A potter can take a chunk of clay and turn it into something amazing. With a little push here and a little pull there, they shape the clay. Their hands keep working until the design is finished and it's just what they want it to be.

Imagine you are that hunk of clay, and God is the Potter. He's molding, pushing, pulling, and making you into who he wants you to be. Sometimes he shapes you with a Bible verse, a friendship, an opportunity to help, or a chance to tell others about him. God will even use the hard times, the troubles, and the challenges to mold you and teach you to trust him.

God never stops working on you. He never stops shaping your life. He knows what he's doing, and he's got a plan to make you look more and more like him.

Will you still mess up and make mistakes? Of course! You're human. But you're also a wonderful work in progress. God started this good work in you before you were even born, and he'll keep working on you your whole life long.

No matter what is happening in the world around you or in your life, you can trust that God will use it for your good (Romans 8:28-29). So you never have to worry . . . because you're in good hands.

Read All About It

Read more about the Potter in Isaiah 45 and Isaiah 64:8.

Talk About It

If you have some Play-Doh, pull it out and begin stretching and shaping it. Imagine if that Play-Doh had feelings. Would all that stretching and shaping feel good? Now, remember that God the Potter is stretching and shaping you. Will it always feel good? Why is it sometimes hard to be stretched and shaped by God?

Pray About It

God, thank you for working on us and making us more and more like Jesus. Please help us to be easy to shape into who you want us to be. Amen.

Let's Do This

God shaped you as a one-of-a-kind original, and his fingerprints are all over you. To see just how original you are, grab a washable ink pad, press your finger into the ink, and then gently press it onto a piece of paper. Have family members or friends do the same. Examine the prints and how different they are—then praise God for making you each so amazing!

Go Bigger

Play a game of Pictionary Play-Doh! Write down ten to twenty simple objects on slips of paper, such as *ball*, *spaghetti*, *flower*, *pizza*, and *house*. Fold the papers and put them in a cup. One person is the Potter and chooses a slip of paper. They then have one minute to shape a hunk of Play-Doh into the object on the paper while everyone else guesses what it is. The first to guess gets to be the next Potter.

A Perfect World

In this world, there are terrible storms, itchy weeds, and animals that bite—and that doesn't include all the sickness and disease. But that's not how God created it to be.

When God first made the world, it was perfect in every way. It was exactly how he wanted it to be. But then . . . Adam and Eve ate the one fruit God told them not to eat. That's when sin came into the world and everything changed.

We usually think about how sin affected God's people and brought sadness, anger, hurt, and hatred into our lives. But sin did more than that. It took away the perfection of God's creation. It brought poison, rot, and disease to plants. Animals began to hunt each other and learned to be afraid. Storms and disasters of every kind became part of our planet. Sin didn't just mess things up for people—it messed things up for all of God's creation.

But one day, after Jesus returns to earth, sin will all be gone—and so will all those other hurtful, harmful things.

God will create new heavens and a new earth where everything will be exactly as he wants it to be. No more sadness or storms. No more death or disease. No more anger or hurt. Wolves will nap with lambs! Lions will munch on hay! And that's where we'll live with God, in a perfect world of love and joy and light . . . forever.

Read All About It

Read more about the new heavens and earth in Isaiah 65:17-25.

Talk About It

Revelation 21:4 says God "will wipe every tear from their eyes, and there will be no more death or sorrow or crying or pain." Revelation 22:5 says there will be no more darkness. Talk about all the things we'll never need again in God's perfect world, like hospitals, bandages, and flashlights!

Pray About It

Lord, we can't wait to see your new heavens and earth. Thank you for sending Jesus to make a way for us to be with you forever. Amen.

Let's Do This

You can't make this world perfect—only God can do that. But you can make it better. Do something to make this world a little better today, like pick up some trash, be kind, or leave a note for your parents telling them how awesome they are.

Go Bigger

One of the best things you can do to make this world a better place is to pray. With your family, take a prayer walk around your neighborhood, street, school, or church. Ask God to bless and protect the people there. Most importantly, ask him to help them get to know him.

A Fiery Choice

If we are thrown into the blazing furnace, the God whom we serve is able to save us. He will rescue us from your power, Your Majesty.

DANIEL 3:17

Have you ever been laughed at for doing the right thing? Or for standing up to someone who's doing the wrong thing? Or because you chose to follow God?

Shadrach, Meshach, and Abednego faced something far worse than being laughed at or picked on. For them, it was a life-or-death situation.

Years before, these three Israelites had been taken as captives to Babylon. Now they were trusted officials in King Nebuchadnezzar's government there. Until one day when the king ordered all his officials to bow down to the massive, ninety-foot-tall golden statue he had built. Anyone who didn't would be thrown into a fiery furnace.

Everyone bowed down. Except Shadrach, Meshach, and Abednego.

"We will never serve your gods or worship the gold statue you have set up," they declared, and they trusted God to take care of them (Daniel 3:18).

The king was furious. He ordered his servants to make the furnace even hotter and then throw the three men inside!

But when the king looked into the flames, the men were walking around, unharmed. And he saw a fourth man with them who looked like an angel from God!

"Come out!" the king called. Shadrach, Meshach, and Abednego stepped out. They didn't even smell like smoke. They trusted God to take care of them—and he did!

Today, if you stand up for God and what's right, you probably

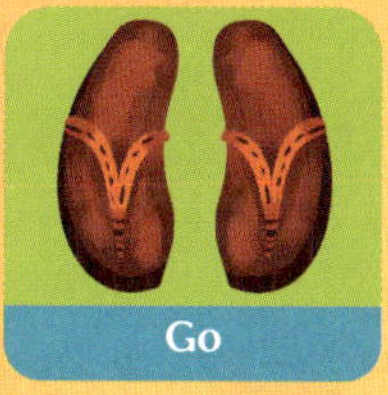

won't be tossed into a fiery furnace, but you might be laughed at or lose some friends.

Be bold anyway! Stand up for what's right anyway. Follow God anyway. He was with those guys in the fire—and he'll be with you.

Read All About It

Read more about Shadrach, Meshach, and Abednego in Daniel 3.

Talk About It

Have you even been laughed at, left out—or worse—because you love God and choose to do what is right? Read Matthew 5:10-12. What does Jesus say about being mocked and made fun of for following Jesus? How could it be a blessing?

Pray About It

Lord, help us not to worry about whether people laugh or make fun. Instead, give us the courage to speak up for you every chance we get. Amen.

Let's Do This

The actions of Shadrach, Meshach, and Abednego sent a message loud and clear: They loved, trusted, and followed God. Do your actions tell the world who you love, trust, and follow? Next time someone asks you to do something that would not be pleasing to God, be prepared to stand up for what's right.

Go Bigger

Bold faith starts with knowing the God you have faith in. Get to know God better by committing to read a passage from the Bible every day together as a family. You can simply dive in and begin with Genesis or perhaps Matthew in the New Testament. Or you can ask a grown-up to help you find a reading plan.

47

The God of Second Chances

Be kind to each other, tenderhearted, forgiving one another, just as God through Christ has forgiven you.

EPHESIANS 4:32

Imagine what would happen if . . .

You wrecked your brother's bike and scratched it all up. But it was an accident, so he would understand, right? Even though you didn't speak to him for a week when he messed up your video game.

Or maybe you came in from school starving. So you scarfed down the last piece of your sister's birthday cake, even though you heard her say she was saving it for herself. But you were hungry, right? She can just find something else to snack on, you think.

Or your best friend went off with some other friends and didn't invite you, so you refused to sit with her at lunch or even look at her. She tried to apologize and explain, but you wouldn't even stop to listen. Even though, a couple of weeks ago, you went to hang out with some other friends and didn't invite her.

Do any of those situations sound right or fair?

When we mess up, we expect others to give us grace—to give us a second chance. And it *is* good to give others grace. The question is, though, do we offer others a second chance when they mess up? Or do we get angry and upset instead?

God is so generous with his grace. He doesn't just give us a second chance. God gives us a third, fourth, and 387th chance. When we tell him we're sorry for our mistakes, he is always ready to forgive.

Make it your goal to be as generous with your grace and forgiveness as God is with his.

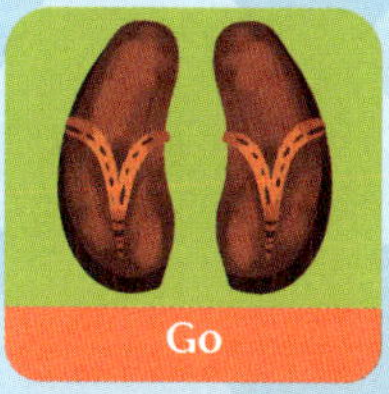

Read All About It

Read more about how God gave his people a second chance in Hosea 11:1-11.

Talk About It

Some things are big and hurtful and hard to forgive. It may take time, and there may still be consequences. Because forgiving someone doesn't mean what they did was okay. Why are some things harder to forgive than others? What can you do when you're struggling to forgive?

Pray About It

Lord, you are so generous with your grace and forgive all our sins. Help us not to be stingy with our forgiveness of others. Amen.

Let's Do This

God loves to give us second chances when we ask him. But is it easy for you to give second chances? Is there someone you need to forgive? Ask God to help you.

Go Bigger

Families spend a lot of time together. We can get in the habit of being kinder and more forgiving to other people than we are to those closest to us. Make this week Family Kindness Week. Do something extra kind every day for each person in your family. It can be as simple as taking out the trash without being told, or it can be something bigger like making them a special gift, just because.

A Mission for You

Love each other. Just as I have loved you, you should love each other. Your love for one another will prove to the world that you are my disciples.

JOHN 13:34-35

God had a mission for Jonah: Go to the city of Nineveh. Tell them that God had seen their wickedness and was about to punish them.

Jonah didn't want to go. He knew that if the people of Nineveh heard that message, they might turn back to God, and God would give them another chance. But the people of Nineveh were so wicked, Jonah didn't think they deserved a second chance.

Jonah was making a decision that wasn't his to make.

God's promises aren't just for people who look and live like us. They're available to everyone—every nation and race, boys and girls, women and men, young and old, rich and poor. God loves everyone. He gives everyone a chance to turn away from their sins and wickedness and turn to him. God wants *everyone* to be part of his family.

All those years ago, God even gave Jonah a second chance to do the right thing. Jonah went to Nineveh, though he wasn't happy about it. And God used him to get the people of Nineveh to turn away from their sins.

Today, God wants to send you on a mission to spread his message too. (Though he hopes you'll be happier about it than Jonah was!) You can start right where you are by choosing to see every person—yes, even those who are very different from you—as someone God loves. You'll soon discover that the more you love others, the more you love him too.

Read All About It

Read more about Jonah and God's mission for him in Jonah 1–4.

Talk About It

Read through Matthew 1 and check out all the different people in Jesus' family tree. There were people from different cultures, like Ruth and Rahab. There were people who made mistakes and people who tried to do what was right. Talk about how there's room for all people in God's family. How can you make everyone feel welcome?

Pray About It

Lord, help us to see each and every person—especially those who are different from us—as someone you created and love. And help us to love them too. Amen.

Let's Do This

As you go through your day, notice all the people you meet and how very different we all are. Then remember the one thing that makes us all the same: Each and every one was created in the image of God and is dearly loved by him.

Go Bigger

One way to appreciate how wonderful people from all cultures are is to learn more about their customs. Go out to a restaurant from a different culture, one you've never tried before. Look around. What do their decorations and art tell you about their culture? Do they have special customs for eating and serving food? Then everyone can pick a different dish and dive in!

Not So Bad?

We compare ourselves to others in so many ways, don't we? *I'm taller than he is. She's faster than I am. I've got better grades. His clothes are cooler. I'm more popular.* Those comparisons can make us feel better—or worse!—about ourselves, and it's something we need to be careful about doing. Because we're all originals in our own wonderful ways.

But there's one kind of comparison we definitely need to avoid. That's comparing our sins to the sins of others. *I'm not as bad as she is. I don't do the stuff he does. I may mess up, but I've never acted like that!*

The trouble with this kind of comparison is that we start to think the sinful things we do and say aren't really *that* bad. So maybe we don't have to worry about changing our ways. *Wrong!*

There's only one person we need to compare ourselves to: Jesus.

Stop and think about that for a minute. How do you measure up when you compare yourself to the Son of God, who never once sinned? That's the comparison that will show you how much you need God and his grace.

No matter how big or small, how bad or not-so-bad our sins are, we deserve to be punished for them all. But God is kinder and more loving than we could ever imagine. That's why he sent Jesus.

We don't need to compare ourselves to others to feel better about who we are. We just need to follow Jesus so we can be forgiven and so we can be his.

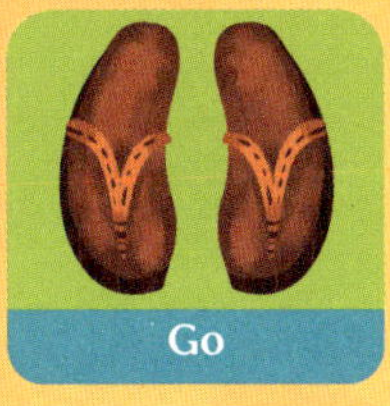

Read All About It

Read more about God's warnings to his people about sin in Zephaniah 1.

Talk About It

Romans 3:23 says, "Everyone has sinned; we all fall short of God's glorious standard." In other words, we all need God. So why do we compare our sins to the sins of others? Why do we try to make ourselves feel "not so bad"? What should we do instead?

Pray About It

God, we do love you! Please forgive us for the times we sin. Help us to follow your commands. Amen.

Let's Do This

Imagine this: You're driving along in a car. You see a red light, but you decide to zoom right through it. The road was empty, and you didn't hurt anyone, but you still broke the law, right? How is that like sin? Sin might not hurt anyone else, but it's still wrong, and it will always hurt your friendship with God.

Go Bigger

Take turns testing your Bible knowledge with this twist on Simon Says. If what "Simon" says is true, stand up. If it's false, sit down. Here are some sample statements to get you started. Then make up more of your own.

- Adam and Eve got to stay in the garden of Eden forever. (false)
- Everyone sins and makes mistakes. (true)
- If we ask God to forgive us, he will. (true)
- If we mess up one time, God is done with us. (false)
- Jesus came to die to take the punishment for our sins. (true)

God's Got a Plan

> We can make our plans, but the LORD determines our steps.
>
> PROVERBS 16:9

When was the last time you—or your friends, or maybe your family—made a plan? It could have been a plan to finish a group science project, a plan for your next vacation, or a plan to fix a problem.

Once you set out to accomplish your plan, did everything go exactly the way you hoped? Probably not. Because we're not perfect, our plans aren't going to be either.

Yet when a problem pops into our lives, we still like to make a plan to fix it. And then we kind of expect God to follow *our* plan. When he doesn't, we might start to wonder why. We might start to wonder if he's paying attention or if he really cares. The answer to both of those questions is yes. Yes, God is paying attention and sees what's going on. And yes, he really does care. He's just not following *our* plan.

That's because unlike us, God is perfect, and he's got perfect knowledge of the past, present, and future. So he knows exactly what we need and when we need it. God's not following our plan because he's got a better one. It might not look like the one we came up with, and it might take us in unexpected directions. But it will be the perfect plan for us.

It's time to stop trying to fix everything ourselves and trust God instead. He promises to take care of us. And that's exactly what he'll do with *his* perfect plan.

Read All About It

Read more about God's plans in Jeremiah 29:11 and Proverbs 16:9.

Talk About It

Proverbs 16:9 says, "We can make our plans, but the LORD determines our steps." What does this mean? Whose plans always work out? Why do we struggle to give up our own plans?

Pray About It

Lord, when we don't understand what's going on in this world, remind us that you have good and perfect plans for our lives. And help us to trust and keep following you. Amen.

Let's Do This

God knows the past, the present, the future, and everything about you. What does that tell you about the kind of plans he has for you?

Go Bigger

Draw the story of your life! Start with the day you were born. Include a picture of when you were a toddler and another of when you first started school. Add any favorite memories or events. Now, add what's going to happen next year. *What's that? You don't know the future?* You don't know the future, but God does! And you can trust that he's got it all perfectly planned out for you.

51

A Really Good Thing

> Don't copy the behavior and customs of this world, but let God transform you into a new person by changing the way you think. Then you will learn to know God's will for you, which is good and pleasing and perfect.
>
> ROMANS 12:2

Wearing scratchy camel's-hair clothes, munching on locusts, and challenging all the people in charge, John the Baptist definitely didn't blend in with the crowd.

John the Baptist was Jesus' cousin and just a few months older than him. John had been sent by God as a messenger to tell the world that the Messiah—the Savior, Jesus—was coming, so they'd better get ready. How should they get ready? John told the people to confess the things they'd done wrong and be baptized in the Jordan River to show that they had turned away from sin.

The Jewish religious leaders didn't like what John was preaching, though (see Luke 7:30). They didn't like that he was teaching about God—that was their business, and they liked being the bosses of it! They also thought John was weird and strange and perhaps even out of his mind. And they weren't the only ones. Plenty of other people thought so too.

But John was doing exactly what God wanted him to do. And plenty of people were listening and changing their lives because of the message he shared.

When you decide to follow Jesus, you won't blend in with this world either. That's because you'll be doing things God's way instead of doing what's easy and popular. Some people might even think you're weird or strange. But you know what? That's not just a good thing . . . it's a *really* good thing (check out Romans 12:2).

Read All About It
Read more about John the Baptist in Matthew 3.

Talk About It
Have you ever done anything silly or maybe just plain wrong to try to fit in? As a family, talk about some of these things—and what you would do differently if you could.

Pray About It
God, help us not to worry about fitting in with this world. Instead, show us how to stand out for you. Amen.

Let's Do This
John the Baptist told the people to repent. *Repent* means to turn away from your sins and turn back to God and to living his way. Ask God to show you if there is anything you need to repent of.

Go Bigger
John the Baptist came to prepare the people's hearts and minds for the coming of Jesus. This week, gather as a family the day or night before church to prepare your hearts and minds to worship Jesus. If possible, reach out to your pastor to see what he'll be teaching. Read the passage, pray, and sing—and get ready to meet Jesus in church.

Are You Stuck?

One day, Jesus was teaching in a house. Crowds of people gathered to hear him, including some Pharisees and teachers of the law.

Some men came carrying their friend on a mat because he could not walk. His friends hoped Jesus would heal him, but so many people were packed inside the house that they couldn't even get in the door.

Instead of giving up, they climbed onto the roof, ripped a hole in it, and lowered their friend down—right in front of Jesus!

Jesus saw the friends' faith and said, "Young man, your sins are forgiven" (Luke 5:20).

The Pharisees and teachers of the law were furious. "Who does he think he is?" they said to themselves. "Only God can forgive sins!" (5:21).

Jesus knew what they were thinking, though. "I will prove to you that the Son of Man has the authority on earth to forgive sins," he said. "Stand up, pick up your mat, and go home!" (5:24).

The man jumped up, picked up his mat, and praised God all the way home! Everyone was amazed.

That paralyzed man was stuck on his mat until Jesus changed his life. But he wasn't the only "stuck" person in that room. The Pharisees and teachers of the law were also stuck . . . in pride and anger. Jesus would have changed their lives too—if they had just asked.

Do you ever feel stuck? Stuck in a friendship that isn't good for you? Stuck in habits you know are wrong? Stuck in selfishness? You don't have to stay stuck. Jesus can change your life too. Just ask.

Read All About It

Read more about the paralyzed man in Luke 5:17-26.

Talk About It

In Bible times, people often blamed sickness and injuries on something bad a person—or even their parents—had done. So in addition to being paralyzed, this man was probably looked down on and whispered about as people wondered what his sin was. How do you think that made him feel? Why was forgiving his sins a greater gift than healing his legs?

Pray About It

Lord, forgive us for the times our hearts are hard like those Pharisees. Change us and make us more and more like you. Amen.

Let's Do This

That man on the mat had good friends who carried him where he needed to go. But the greatest thing they did for him was to carry him to Jesus. Today, take a few minutes to "carry" your friends to Jesus in prayer.

Go Bigger

Gather friends and family, and set up an obstacle course in your house or in the backyard. Have one person lie down on a blanket while the others carry them through the obstacle course. Take turns being the person on the mat. Set a timer and see which group can do it the fastest—without dropping the friend on the mat!

53

The Prayers God Loves to Answer

We are confident that he hears us whenever we ask for anything that pleases him. And since we know he hears us when we make our requests, we also know that he will give us what we ask for.

1 JOHN 5:14-15

Wait, did that verse at the top just say that God will give us what we ask for? Well, yes and no. Read it again, but this time pay special attention to the first sentence. See that part that says, "whenever we ask for anything that pleases him"? That's the key.

The more time you spend with God—talking to him, worshiping him, and reading his words in the Bible—the better you'll get to know him. Your heart will start to look more and more like his. Then you'll begin to want more and more of the things he wants. That's when your prayers will change.

You might notice that your prayers are changing already. How? Here's a hint: Your prayers will be less and less about the stuff of this world, like a new bike, the latest game, or getting to be part of the popular crowd. Instead, you'll be asking him for things like helping you tell someone about him, forgive others, and love your enemies.

God hears every single prayer you pray, and he answers them all too. Because he knows everything, his answers will always be perfect for you. Sometimes God says *no*. It might be because he knows the thing you're asking for isn't quite right for you, or God might say *no* for a reason you won't understand until you meet him face-to-face one day. Other times, God's answer is *wait* because he has something even better planned for you.

But when your heart looks more like God's heart and you begin to pray for the things he wants too, that's when God loves to say *yes* to you.

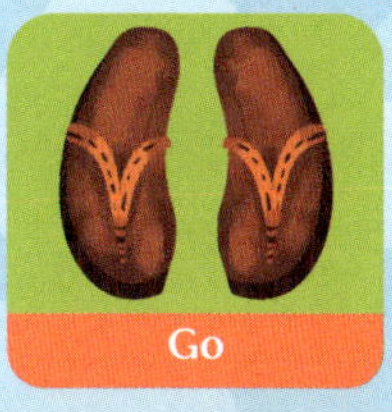

Read All About It

Read more about prayer in Matthew 6:9-13 and 1 John 5:14-15.

Talk About It

There are some prayers God loves to say *yes* to. Each line of the Lord's Prayer in Matthew 6:9-13 contains an example. What requests are found in the Lord's Prayer? Why does God love to answer *yes* to them? Are there other prayers God loves to say *yes* to? (Hint: Find one in James 1:5.)

Pray About It

God, please change our hearts so that we want the same things as you. Draw us closer and closer to you each day. Amen.

Let's Do This

When you're not quite sure what to pray, remember to CHAT with God. CHAT stands for *C*onfess, *H*onor, *A*sk, and *T*hank.

Go Bigger

Create a family prayer wall on your refrigerator, on a poster board—or anywhere everyone will see it. Give each person a different color of sticky note to write their prayer requests on. Stick them on the prayer wall and pray over them each time you pass by. Move answered prayers to a special "Praise" spot.

What's the Big Deal?

> The gateway to life is very narrow and the road is difficult, and only a few ever find it.
>
> MATTHEW 7:14

Everybody's watching *that* show. Everybody's singing along to *that* song. Everybody's saying *those* words.

So what's the big deal? If everybody's doing it, it must be okay, right? Wrong! Jesus said doing what everyone else does is like walking through a wide gate. *It's easy*. You don't even have to think. Just follow the crowd and do whatever they do. But that "gate"—that way of living—leads straight to destruction and the evil one!

There's only one way into God's Kingdom, and that's through the "narrow gate" of following Jesus. That means choosing to do what he does. Like choosing to be kind when others aren't. Choosing to love and help when others choose to hate and hurt. And choosing to forgive when others choose to hold a grudge or get even.

Not many people live their lives that way. So when you follow Jesus, you're going to be different. That's why Jesus called it the narrow gate. To be honest, it can be tough sometimes. You can't just do what everyone else does. You'll have to think about your choices, the words you use, and the things you do. You'll need to pray and talk to God. You'll need the wisdom from his Word and plenty of courage.

There might be times when it seems impossible. Don't worry, though. Jesus will help you—and he's really good at making impossible things possible!

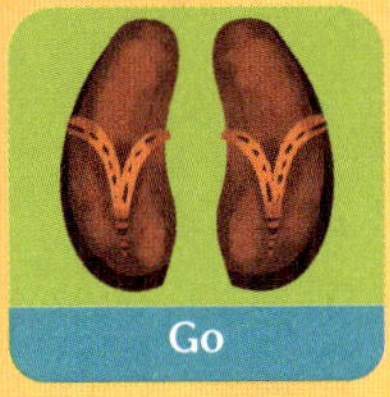

Read All About It

Read more about Nicodemus's visit to Jesus in John 3:1-21.

Talk About It

Jesus was both fully God and fully human. Talk about how Jesus grew up just like us. What ordinary things would he have done? How could growing up and living like us help Jesus to understand our struggles? How would that help him to know what we need?

Pray About It

Father God, there aren't enough words to tell you how grateful we are that you sent your Son to save us. Please help us to live lives that show the world how wonderful you are. Amen.

Let's Do This

Every verse in the Bible is important because every verse is the inspired Word of God, which means that God gave his words to the writers to record on paper. But one of the most important verses is John 3:16. Memorize John 3:16 and hide it away in your heart.

Go Bigger

Choose a night to gather with those you love to act out the story of John 3:1-21 in the way it would have really happened. Ahead of time, set up a room with a Bible open to John 3. Turn off all the lights. Begin at your front door and, using a candle to light the way, have everyone make their way through darkness—like Nicodemus would have done—to the room where the Bible is. Share the story, and then share your praises to God.

56

Watch Out for Wolves!

> Beware of false prophets who come disguised as harmless sheep but are really vicious wolves.
>
> MATTHEW 7:15

Have you ever heard of a wolf in sheep's clothing? This is a person who pretends to be good and kind and helpful, but they're actually out to tear you down.

Jesus and his disciples talked about some wolves in sheep's clothing in the Bible. That's how they described false teachers and false prophets. These people didn't like Jesus' teachings, and they didn't like God's rules, so they made up their own.

There are still plenty of false teachers and prophets today. And they still make up their own teachings. They might say things like, "God just wants us to be happy," as an excuse to do something they know is wrong. These false teachers might even tell you, "That's what the Bible says," when it doesn't really say that at all.

Why do people listen to false teachers? Because they'd rather hear lies that let them do whatever they want to do instead of listening to God's truth (see 2 Timothy 4:3). But God isn't a puppet we can make say whatever we want.

Yes, it's true that God does have rules, but not because he's mean or doesn't want you to have fun. God's rules bring freedom from sin, shame, guilt, and other dangerous things. They help you find joy and peace, and they help you become more and more like him.

How can you spot a false teacher? By comparing what they say to God's true Word. If it doesn't match, run away!

Read All About It

Read more about the dangers of false teachers in Matthew 7:15-20, Matthew 10:16, Acts 20:28-30, and 2 Peter 2:1-2.

Talk About It

False friends—like false teachers—are everywhere. How can you spot them? They're nice to your face but gossip behind your back. They lie and twist the truth. They encourage you to do things you know are wrong. Do you have any experience with false friends? Brainstorm ways to respond to them.

Pray About It

Father God, please protect us from false friends and false teachers. Give us the wisdom to spot their lies and the courage to share your truth. Amen.

Let's Do This

False teachers often use a little bit of God's truth, but they twist it and add a lie. Protect yourself with the sword of the Spirit, also known as the Bible. Find a song that lists the books of the Bible and start memorizing them. Knowing the books of the Bible will help you find verses quickly and be ready to use your sword!

Go Bigger

Secret Service agents learn to recognize counterfeit money by studying real money, not the fake stuff. Put on your investigator's hat and take a look at a real dollar bill. How does it feel and smell? What colors, letters, and numbers are used? Now compare it to a fake dollar. Spot any differences? (PS: That's also the best way to spot false teaching—by knowing the real Bible!)

57

What Kind of Seed Will You Be?

[Jesus] taught them by telling many stories in the form of parables.

MARK 4:2

Jesus was a storyteller. But his stories weren't fairy tales. Jesus told stories called *parables* that taught people about God. He used things they understood—like seeds—to explain things they didn't understand.

For example, some people hear about Jesus and change their whole lives to follow him, while others hear the exact same words but refuse to change. Jesus explained that in a parable about a farmer scattering seeds.

Once, Jesus told the crowd, there was a farmer who scattered seeds across his field. Some fell on the path, and the birds ate them. Other seeds fell on rocky soil. They sprouted quickly but wilted in the hot sun. Some seeds fell into the weeds, and the weeds choked them out. But other seeds fell on good, rich soil. They grew and grew and produced a huge crop.

Jesus' disciples didn't understand his story. So Jesus explained: The seeds on the path are those who hear God's message but don't understand, and the devil snatches the seeds away. The seeds on the rocky soil are those who hear the message and instantly receive it with joy. But because they don't have deep roots, their faith doesn't last when problems come along. The seeds that fall among the weeds are those who hear God's message, but it's quickly choked out by the worries and riches of this world.

Those last seeds that fall on good soil, though, are those who hear and understand God's Word. They live for him, and their lives grow a rich harvest of other people who believe in God.

The question is: What kind of seed will you be?

Read All About It

Read more about the parable of the seeds in Matthew 13:1-23 and Mark 4:1-20.

Talk About It

In the parable, what was the farmer's job? Did he control whether or not the seeds grew? Talk about how our job is to scatter seeds, and God's job is to take care of the soil. Only he can truly change hearts so they're open to his Word.

Pray About It

God, please help the soil of our hearts to be rich and good for growing. And please help us to scatter the seeds of your Word wherever we go. Amen.

Let's Do This

Look for somewhere—or someone—to sow a little seed of God's truth today. When you spot a rainbow, talk about how amazing God's creation is. When someone is worried, remind them that God is always ready to help them, and then pray with them. And if someone is just having a really rotten day, offer a hug and a reminder that God loves them.

Go Bigger

Plant some sunflower seeds in pots. But first, fill one pot with rocks, another with mostly rocks and a little bit of soil, another with grass, and another with good, rich soil. Give each water and sunlight. Do you see any differences in how they grow?

58

No Ordinary Person

> O Sovereign LORD! You made the heavens and earth by your strong hand and powerful arm. Nothing is too hard for you!
>
> JEREMIAH 32:17

Jairus needed a miracle. His daughter was dying, and Jesus was his only hope.

Jairus was a leader in the local synagogue. He was an important man. But he didn't care about any of that. He ran to find Jesus. And when he finally found him, Jairus dropped to his knees in front of Jesus and begged him to come heal his daughter.

Jesus followed the man to his home. When they arrived, the people were weeping and wailing and saying the girl had already died.

Now, people everywhere were saying Jesus could do miracles. But when Jesus told the crowds the little girl was only sleeping, they laughed! They knew she was dead. *Who could bring someone back from death?* they thought. But that's exactly what Jesus did. Because he is the Son of God, and nothing is impossible for him.

Is that ever hard for you to believe? That nothing is impossible for Jesus? Maybe it's when *you* need something impossible, something no ordinary person could do. That's your answer, of course. Jesus isn't an ordinary person. *He's the Son of God.* Nothing is too hard for him.

You can trust Jesus with your impossible problems and your impossible dreams. Why? Because he's impossibly powerful and his love for you is impossibly endless. Ask him to open your eyes to see all the wonderful possibilities of a life lived with him.

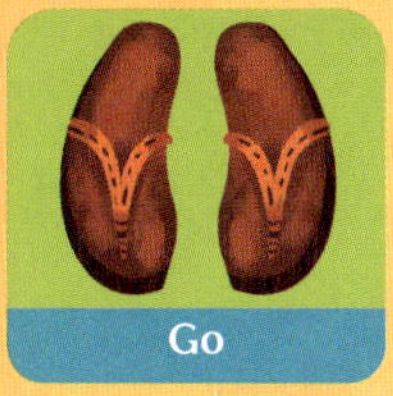

Read All About It

Read more about how Jesus healed Jairus's daughter in Mark 5:21-24, 35-43.

Talk About It

When we think about God doing impossible things, we often picture miracles, like raising Jairus's daughter. But there are an endless number of things that are impossible for us but easy-peasy for God. Like making a person, painting a rainbow across the sky, or tucking an oak tree inside an acorn. How many impossible-for-us but easy-for-God things can you name?

Pray About It

Lord, we know you are working in our lives. Open our eyes to see all the many wonderfully impossible things you do each and every day. Amen.

Let's Do This

Need a reminder that God can do impossible things? Look up at the stars. The God who calls each one of them by name is the same God who knows your name and is looking after you! There's no limit to what he can do.

Go Bigger

Read the story of Jairus's daughter together as a family. Then write out the names of the different people in the story on slips of paper (Jairus, his wife, his daughter, the crowd who laughed, Jesus, and the disciples). Fold the slips and put them in a cup. Have each person draw out a slip and retell the story from that person's point of view—telling the story as that character saw it happen.

59

Lost and Found

The Son of Man came to seek and save those who are lost.

LUKE 19:10

Jesus often spent time with tax collectors and other notorious sinners. He sometimes even shared a meal with them! The Pharisees and other religious leaders thought this was terrible. So Jesus told them a story about a man who had one hundred sheep.

One of the man's sheep wandered away, and he had a choice to make. Should he go after the one lost sheep or just let it go? After all, he still had ninety-nine sheep all safe at home.

What did the man do? He left the ninety-nine and went out to search for his missing sheep. When he found it, he was so happy that he scooped it up and carried it all the way home on his shoulders. Then he celebrated the good news with all his neighbors and friends.

Maybe you're wondering what a lost sheep has to do with eating dinner with sinners. You see, the Pharisees and religious leaders didn't believe the tax collectors and sinners should be part of God's family. They would rather leave those sinners to be lost like that one sheep.

But not Jesus. He loves every single person—every single sheep. And when one of them is lost in sin, he goes after them. He searches and searches until he finds them. Then he joyfully scoops them up on his shoulders and brings them home into his family.

That's important because, at one time or another, we're all that lost sheep. We all need Jesus to come after and rescue us. Thankfully, that's what he came to do.

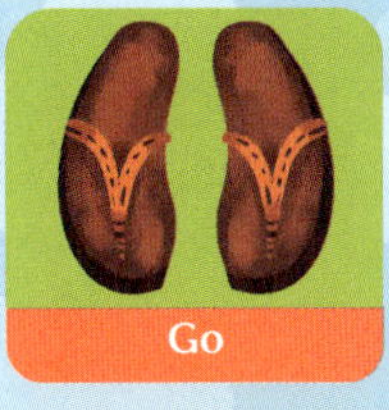

Read All About It

Read more about the lost sheep in Matthew 18:12-14 and Luke 15:1-7.

Talk About It

Have you ever lost something you didn't really care about? Maybe a pencil or a sock? You probably didn't waste much time looking for it. But what if you lose something important—like a favorite game or your homework? You search until you find it, right? Read Luke 19:10. What is Jesus' mission? How important are lost people to him? How long will he search for them?

Pray About It

God, thank you for loving each and every one of us. Please teach us how to show your love and saving power to those who are lost. Amen.

Let's Do This

Think of some things you've searched for. How did you feel if you found it? How did you feel if you didn't? How do you think Jesus feels when someone who is lost turns back and decides to follow him?

Go Bigger

Play an epic game of hide-and-seek with your family and friends. Choose one person to be the seeker while everyone else—the sheep—hides. Each time a person is found they become a seeker too. After all, that's what Jesus wants his followers to do . . . help him seek and find the lost.

Hosanna!

At the name of Jesus every knee should bow, in heaven and on earth and under the earth, and every tongue declare that Jesus Christ is Lord, to the glory of God the Father.

PHILIPPIANS 2:10-11

It was time for the Passover feast, and Jesus was returning to Jerusalem. He knew it was dangerous. He knew the religious leaders were looking for him. And he knew they wanted to find a way to kill him. But Jesus came anyway.

Crowds of people came down to the road to meet him and worship him with their praises. They had heard about all the miracles Jesus had done—healing the sick, making the blind see, and even raising Lazarus up from the grave (see John 11:1-44). Though they didn't fully understand why Jesus had come, they knew he was there to give them hope.

When Jesus arrived, he came riding into Jerusalem on a young donkey, just like the long-ago prophecies said he would. The crowds called out to him, "Hosanna!" They spread palm branches on the road in front of him and cheered, "Hail to the King of Israel" (John 12:13).

Hosanna! means "Praise God!" in Greek. It also sounds like a Hebrew term that means "Save now!" The people praised Jesus with this word because they hoped he would save them from their enemies and foreign rulers: the Romans. They didn't understand that Jesus came to save them from the even bigger enemies of sin and death.

In this world, we praise a lot of people and things—from sports players and movie stars to our family, friends, and even pets. But there is only one who deserves to be *worshiped* with our praise: Jesus. Because he's the one who saves us. *Hosanna!*

Read All About It

Read more about Jesus' journey into Jerusalem in John 12:12-17.

Talk About It

Who do you praise? Is it people in your family? Friends? Or someone out in the world, like a sports star or famous actor? It's fine to admire people and think they are wonderful. But only Jesus is worthy of our worship. Why is that? What makes Jesus different? Why is it sometimes so easy to praise the people and things of this world, but harder to remember to praise Jesus?

Pray About It

Lord, you are the only one worthy of our worship and praise. We bow before you and thank you for who you are and all you do in our lives. Amen.

Let's Do This

What's your favorite praise song? Sing it today—out loud or just in your heart. Don't know all the words? Look them up and start memorizing them.

Go Bigger

Have a family concert of praise! Sing all your favorite praise songs. Take turns leading and choosing songs to sing. Add to the joy by inviting others to join you.

When You're Angry

Don't sin by letting anger control you.

EPHESIANS 4:26

Jesus was angry!

People in the Temple were buying and selling doves and other animals for sacrifice. Money changers were there, too, swapping the people's money for Temple coins. And they were all cheating God's people!

Jesus burst in. He knocked over tables, tossed aside chairs, and drove out the people selling animals. Coins rolled across the floor, sheep baaed, doves flew every which way, and people scattered!

Does that surprise you? That Jesus was angry and did all that? Because Jesus never sinned, right? Right! It wasn't a sin for Jesus to be angry, and it wasn't a sin for him to toss those tables. What made his anger and his actions okay? Because Jesus was angry about something that was wrong, and his actions were to make that wrong right.

It's okay get angry. It was okay for Jesus, and it's okay for you. It's what we do *after* we get angry that matters. Sometimes we need to just let it go. Like when we're upset over a mistake we made or frustrated because we don't want to share.

But when we're angry because someone hurt us, didn't respect God, or did something God says is wrong, that's called *righteous anger*—it means we're right to be angry. That's the kind of anger Jesus had when he cleared out the Temple.

The next time you get angry, stop and talk to God. Ask him to show you if your anger is right or wrong and what to do with it. Because you want to be righteous, not wrong!

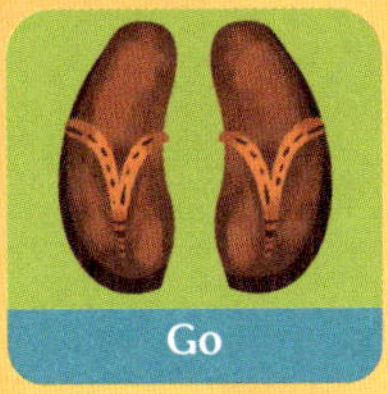

Read All About It

Read more about how Jesus cleared out the Temple in Matthew 21:12-17.

Talk About It

It's not wrong to get angry. But we need to be careful and not let anger turn into sin. What are some things that make you angry? Are any of these things righteous anger? How can you handle your anger so that it doesn't turn into sin?

Pray About It

God, when we get angry, help us to remember to stop and talk to you about it. Give us the wisdom to not let our anger turn into sin. Amen.

Let's Do This

It's important to control your anger and not let your anger control you. Think about that. Are there times when anger—even righteous anger—makes you feel out of control? Ask God to help you.

Go Bigger

Some people get angry and let their anger spew all over everyone around them. That anger can get on others and make them angry too!

To get a feeling for what that's like, take an unopened bottle of soda outside. Take turns shaking it up. Loosen the cap . . . and watch it burst out!

Blowing up with anger isn't healthy. Instead, go for a walk, listen to music, draw or write it out, talk to an adult you trust, and definitely talk to God. Just don't let your anger spew!

You're Invited!

Don't you love getting invitations? Whether it's to a party, a picnic, or a day at the park, it's wonderful to be wanted and included, isn't it?

Well, God is inviting you to something better than any party, picnic, or park. Jesus tells us about it in a parable—a story—about a great feast.

One day, Jesus told his listeners, there was a man who prepared a great feast. He sent out invitations to all his neighbors and friends. When the feast was ready, he sent a servant to tell the guests it was time to come. But one by one they began making excuses.

One man had to check out the field he'd just bought, so he couldn't come. Another wanted to try out his new oxen. Still another had just gotten married.

When the servant told all this to his master, the master was furious! "Go into the town, and invite all the poor, crippled, blind, and lame," he said.

But there was still room for more. So he sent his servant out into the country to invite everyone he could find. The man wanted his house to be full!

That man is like God. He wants his house to be full. Everyone—absolutely everyone—is invited. Don't worry, though. You don't need fancy clothes or a perfect life to attend. It's a "come as you are" party because God loves you just as you are! If you accept God's invitation by believing in his Son, he'll serve you a feast of love, forgiveness, and joy.

Read All About It

Read more about the great feast in Luke 14:15-24.

Talk About It

Everyone, from every nation and tribe in the world, is invited to God's great feast. One day, we'll get to join him there. Even now, God invites us to "feast" on the goodness of his Word. But how often do we make excuses? How often do we say we're too busy or we'll do it after work or school? How can we stop making excuses and dive into God's Word?

Pray About It

Lord, you always have room at your table and in your family for one more. Help us to make room for others too—in our hearts, in our circle of friends, and in our home. Amen.

Let's Do This

If you were throwing a party, who would you invite? Who would you not invite? Think about how God invites even those people to join his great feast and to be part of his family. Does that change who you would include on your invitation list?

Go Bigger

Host a feast as a family. It could be as simple as cookies and cups of water or as fancy as a sit-down meal. It could be for your family, your friends, or your church group. But don't just invite those you know. Invite at least one or more people you don't know very well to come to your feast.

63

Don't Forget to Say Thank You

Give thanks for everything to God the Father in the name of our Lord Jesus Christ.

EPHESIANS 5:20

Jesus was walking toward Jerusalem one day when ten men came out to meet him. These men had leprosy—a terrible skin disease. This disease meant they had to stay far away from other people. They couldn't live with their families, go to the marketplace, or worship in the synagogue. No hanging out with friends. No hugs. And no cure.

When those men saw Jesus coming, they knew he was their only hope. "Jesus, Master, have mercy on us!" they called (Luke 17:13).

And Jesus did. "Go show yourselves to the priests," he said (17:14). Because if the priests said they were healed, they could return to their families and friends.

The men ran toward town, where the priests were. As they ran, they were healed!

One of the men looked down at his hands and feet and saw that he had been healed. He turned, ran back to Jesus, dropped to the ground at Jesus' feet, and thanked him. (This man was a Samaritan. At that time, Jews and Samaritans hated each other. They didn't usually help each other or say thank you!)

"Didn't I heal ten men?" Jesus asked. "Where are the other nine?" (17:17).

Where *were* the other nine? Why didn't they go back to thank Jesus? Maybe they were so excited they forgot. Maybe they were rushing to the priests like Jesus told them to do. Or maybe they thought they deserved to be healed. Whatever the reason, ten were healed. But only one said thank you.

Thanking God is more than good manners. It a way of declaring he is God and worshiping him. Be like the one and remember to thank God.

Read All About It

Read more about the ten lepers in Luke 17:11-19.

Talk About It

Think about those lepers in today's story. Why would only one rush back to say thank you? Could it be that the other nine lepers felt like they deserved the healing? Were they so happy to be healed that they forgot the One who healed them? Or could it be that the Samaritan—who was probably used to being looked down on by Jewish people—realized how great a gift he had been given? What do we forget to thank Jesus for?

Pray About It

Father God, please forgive us when we are like the nine lepers and forget to thank you. Every good and wonderful thing in our lives is from you, and we thank you for them all! Amen.

Let's Do This

Do you forget to say thank you? Make it your mission to say thank you at least ten times today—bonus points if it's to ten different people. And be sure to thank God for filling your life with so many reasons to say thanks!

Go Bigger

Write thank-you notes to your pastor, Sunday school teachers, and others at church. Don't forget those who work behind the scenes where most people don't see all that they do—like the audiovisual team, secretary, classroom helpers, and those who keep the church tidy and clean.

64

What Can You Give?

Give, and you will receive. Your gift will return to you in full—pressed down, shaken together to make room for more, running over, and poured into your lap.

LUKE 6:38

One day, Jesus was sitting outside the Temple watching as people dropped money into the collection box. This money was their gift to God.

Jesus watched ordinary people drop in their coins and walk away. He watched the rich people who made sure their coins landed with a loud clatter so everyone would know they gave *a lot*. And then he watched a poor widow quietly step up and drop in just two small coins. They barely made any sound at all.

But Jesus said: "This poor widow has given more than all the others" (Mark 12:43).

How could she have given *more* when she only gave two small coins? Because, Jesus said, she "has given everything she had to live on" (12:44).

You see, when the other people gave their money, they still had plenty left over. They could still buy the food they needed. But not the widow. She gave all that she had, and then she trusted God to take care of her.

Have you ever noticed how people who have the least often give the most? Maybe it's because they understand what it's like not to have enough. Maybe it's because they've discovered the joy they get when they give to others. And maybe it's because they know they can trust God to give them everything they really need. You can too.

Here's the thing about giving to God: You can never outgive him. He'll always give you more. Sometimes in money, but always in the much more wonderful treasures of his love and joy.

Read All About It

Read more about giving in Mark 12:41-44.

Talk About It

Imagine for a minute what happened to that widow who gave God everything she had to live on. Think of all the times in the Bible when God took care of those who loved him, like Esther, Ruth, Abraham, and David. How do you think God might have taken care of this poor widow?

Pray About It

Father, every good thing we have is a gift from you. Please help us be generous and share. Not because we have to, but for the joy of helping someone you love. Amen.

Let's Do This

Maybe you're thinking, *I'm a kid! What can I give?* Giving doesn't have to be money. It can be time, or help, or prayers. Help an elderly neighbor sweep their porch, read a story to a little brother or sister, or say a prayer for your mom and dad. Pick a way you can give, and do it today!

Go Bigger

Is there someone who always seems to sit alone at church? Perhaps even an older widow like in today's story? As a family, introduce yourselves and ask if you can sit with them. Maybe even invite them to lunch. Because your time and attention is one of the greatest gifts you can give.

In, Not Of

I am praying not only for these disciples but also for all who will ever believe in me through their message.

JOHN 17:20

Did you know that Jesus prayed for you? Just before he went to the Garden of Gethsemane, before he was arrested, and before he was sent to die on the cross, Jesus prayed. He not only took time to think about all his disciples who were there with him, but he stopped to think about you too—and all those who would believe in him because of the message his disciples shared.

Jesus asked his Father to keep you safe from the evil one. He knew—and still knows—you don't belong to this world any more than he did. He asked God to protect you, keep you close, and help you to love all those who love him.

It's that love for others that will help them see that you belong to Jesus. It's that love that shows you belong to God and his Kingdom—not this world.

You still live in this world, though, and you can't hide from it. In fact, Jesus wants you to go out into the world and tell others about him. He just doesn't want you acting like the people *of* this world when you're out there *in* it. That means you turn away from hateful, hurtful, and selfish things. You choose to help, forgive, and encourage instead. In other words, you love others the way Jesus loves you.

Read All About It

Read more about how Jesus prayed for us in John 17.

Talk About It

As followers of Jesus, what does it mean to be *in* the world but not *of* the world? What would that look like at school, around the neighborhood, on your sports team or at science club, or at church? What would it look like with your family?

Pray About It

God, we do still live in this world. Please forgive us for the times we think more about it than we do about you. Help us, instead, to tell the world about you. Amen.

Let's Do This

Jesus didn't just pray for you that one time all those years ago. Romans 8:34 says that Jesus "is sitting in the place of honor at God's right hand, pleading for us." Jesus is still praying for you. Think about that today and let it make you smile.

Go Bigger

Try this "in but not of" experiment. Pour one cup of oil and one cup of water into a large, clear glass. Give it a stir. Do they mix together? No! Imagine you are the water, and the world is the oil. You can be in the world, but still separate from it, just like the water is separate from the oil in the glass.

Pilate's Choice

They arrested Jesus!

Soldiers came to the garden of Gethsemane in the middle of the night with some of the religious leaders, and they dragged Jesus off to the home of the high priest for an illegal trial. They slapped and spit on the Son of God. And then they hauled him off to stand before Pontius Pilate, the Roman governor.

As Jesus stood there, not saying a word, the religious leaders demanded that Pilate have Jesus killed. They were about to start a riot if Pilate didn't!

Pilate wasn't convinced that Jesus was guilty, but a riot would get him into big trouble with his Roman bosses. So he gave in to the pressure of the leaders' demands. Just to keep the peace, Pilate sentenced Jesus to die.

Pilate was more worried about keeping the peace and making those religious leaders happy than he was about killing an innocent man.

Too often people do the wrong thing because it's easier than standing up to others. They're more worried about what others will say and do than what God says is right.

God wants you to be different. He wants you to be brave. And he wants you to do what is good and right. Will it be easy? Probably not. If it were easy, everyone would do it.

But God doesn't just *want* you to do these things. When you ask him, he'll give you the strength and power and courage to do them.

Read All About It

Read more about Pilate's choice in Matthew 27:11-26.

Talk About It

Peer pressure is a powerful thing, and it doesn't just happen to kids. It happens when the people around you pressure you to do something, no matter what age you are. It could be as simple as pressure to have pizza when you'd really rather eat a burger. Or as serious as pressure to shoplift something just to fit in. When do you feel peer pressure? What would help you be able to stand up to peer pressure?

Pray About It

God, sometimes it's so hard for us to say no to others. Please give us the wisdom to know what to do. We want to please you and not worry about what others think. Amen.

Let's Do This

Dare to stand out from the crowd today. It doesn't have to be in a huge way—though it could be. Ask God to open your eyes to the opportunity and to help you do it.

Go Bigger

Saying no to peer pressure can be tough. It's much easier to do the right thing when you've practiced it ahead of time. Practice by role-playing different ways to say no in situations like these:

- A friend wants you to lie to your parents about what movie you're going to see.
- A bully (or a friend) is demanding to copy your homework.
- Everyone is making fun of a certain kid, and you feel pressured to join in.

Brainstorm other times it's tough to say no, and practice them too.

67

It Is Finished

> This is real love—not that we loved God, but that he loved us and sent his Son as a sacrifice to take away our sins.
>
> 1 JOHN 4:10

After Jesus was arrested, and after Pontius Pilate sentenced him to die, Jesus was taken by soldiers to a place called Golgotha, which means Place of the Skull.

There the soldiers nailed him to a cross and left him to die. They divided up his clothes and threw dice to see who would get his robe. Some of the people watched and laughed and mocked him. Others stood nearby and wept, including his mother Mary, his disciple John, and some of the other women who followed Jesus.

After hours on the cross, Jesus said, "I am thirsty." Somone soaked a sponge in vinegar and offered it to him. Once Jesus tasted it, he said, "It is finished!" Then he bowed his head, gave up his spirit, and died (John 19:28-30).

"It is finished." John tells us those were Jesus' last words before he died. But what was finished? *His mission to save us.*

That mission started before the world began. Before Adam and Eve ever took that first bite of forbidden fruit. It lasted through all the prophets and every moment of the Old Testament. Jesus' mission led him from heaven down to a manger in Bethlehem. And it ended when he died to take the punishment for the whole world's sins—and to open the doors of eternal life to everyone who believes in him.

Jesus declared "It is finished" so that, when we follow him, we can declare sin and death are finished too.

Read All About It

Read more about the sacrifice of Jesus in John 19.

Talk About It

God knew right from the start—before the start, even—that we were going to make mistakes and that we were going to need a Savior. That's why he made a plan—right from the beginning—to send Jesus to save us (see 1 Peter 1:18-20). What does that tell you about God's knowledge? About God's love and power?

Pray About It

Father God, there aren't enough words to thank you for sending Jesus to save us. Help us to love you more and more each day, and help us to say, "It is finished" about the sin in our lives. Amen.

Let's Do This

Is there something you need to say "It is finished" about? A bad habit, a wrong way of thinking, a sin? Ask God to help you be finished with it today.

Go Bigger

Find (or buy) some smooth, flat stones. Clean them and paint them (using acrylic or craft paint) with messages like "Jesus is alive" and "Jesus loves you" or simply with a cross. Once they're dry, tuck them into places around town, church, and school for others to find and remember . . . Jesus is alive!

The Helper

When the Father sends the Advocate as my representative—that is, the Holy Spirit—he will teach you everything and will remind you of everything I have told you.

JOHN 14:26

When Jesus came to earth, he was sometimes called Immanuel, which means "God is with us" (Matthew 1:23). God physically came to live *with* his people! He hugged his mama Mary. He learned to be a carpenter from his earthly father Joseph. He walked beside his friends James and John. He went fishing with Peter. Amazing!

But when Jesus returned to heaven, God gave us a gift even more wonderful than "God with us." And it all started at Pentecost.

In the Old Testament, Pentecost was also called the Festival of Weeks, and it happened fifty days after Passover. People from all over came to Jerusalem to celebrate it.

Before Jesus returned to heaven, he told his disciples that God would be sending them a gift, a Helper—the Holy Spirit. And he told his disciples to stay in Jerusalem until God sent them the gift he had promised (see Acts 1:4). So all the believers were gathered in the same place.

Suddenly there was a sound like a mighty roaring wind from heaven. It filled the room where the believers were. Then what looked like flames of fire appeared over each person's head, and they were filled with the Holy Spirit of God!

They began speaking in languages they'd never spoken before. Crowds came running to see what was happening. When Peter saw them, he began to tell them about Jesus. And everyone heard him in their own language.

God had sent his gift! The Holy Spirit had come to live *with* and *in* his followers to teach, comfort, and help them. And when

we follow Jesus, the Holy Spirit comes to live in us too. And that changes everything!

Read All About It

Read more about Pentecost and the gift of the Holy Spirit in Acts 2:1-40.

Talk About It

As amazing as it was for Jesus to come live on the earth and be Immanuel, God with us, it's even more amazing that the Holy Spirit comes to live inside us! What would it be like to have Jesus right beside you? How is it better to have the Holy Spirit inside you?

Pray About It

God, thank you for the gift of your Holy Spirit. Help us to listen closely to him and all that he teaches us about you. Amen.

Let's Do This

What could be better than having Jesus right beside you every day? How about having his Holy Spirit living inside you and helping you every moment of every day? Think about how wonderful it is to know that you never, ever have to be alone.

Go Bigger

Look up the verses about the Holy Spirit and all he does and will do for us. Make a list of all the things he helps us do. Here are a few verses to start with: John 14:26, John 16:12-15, Acts 1:8, Romans 8:26, and Galatians 5:22-23. What gifts do you find in each of these verses?

69

What Matters to God

> Give your gifts in private, and your Father, who sees everything, will reward you.
>
> MATTHEW 6:4

All those who believed in Jesus gathered together to encourage and help each other. Some of them, like Barnabas, even sold part of their land and gave the money to the apostles to help the poor.

Ananias and his wife, Sapphira, saw people doing that. And they saw how much respect and admiration those people got. So they decided to do the same. But their hearts were full of all the wrong reasons. They just wanted everyone to *think* they were wonderful. That wasn't the only mistake they made either.

When Ananias and Sapphira sold the land, they decided to keep part of the money for themselves. But they lied and told the apostles they were giving them *all* the money. Ananias and Sapphira paid a terrible price for their lies . . . they died!

Have you ever lied or kept a secret to get what you want or to look good in front of others? If we care so much about what others think that we lie, break promises, or are just plain selfish to make ourselves look good, that's a serious problem. Is God going to *zap* you for it like he did Ananias and Sapphira? No! God did that as an example for the early church to show how serious he is about sin—and how important what's in your heart is to him.

God values who we are on the inside. He loves when we tell the truth and do what's right, even if it doesn't look impressive. Don't lie to get what you want. Instead, follow God and share what you have with others—not to make yourself look good, but because you care about them.

Read All About It

Read more about Ananias and Sapphira and the importance of being honest in Acts 5:1-11.

Talk About It

Ananias and Sapphira didn't *have* to sell their property or give away all their money to please God. But they did have to tell the truth.

Are you ever tempted to lie in order to fit in or make yourself look good? Do you ever do the right things but for the wrong reasons? Does God care more about your actions or what's in your heart?

Pray About It

God, please give us generous hearts that want to give, and help us to do it for all the right reasons: to help others and to please you. Amen.

Let's Do This

One way to make sure your heart is in the right place is to make sure no one sees you doing good. So . . . how sneaky can you be? Sneaky good, that is. Do something kind today, but don't let anyone see you. Then talk to God, and thank him for the chance to give back to him.

Go Bigger

Who can you surprise? Pack up a few little treat bags with goodies, such as mini candies, stickers, or pens. Tuck in a note that says, "Jesus loves you!" Then see if you can sneak these gifts to friends, family, or classmates without anyone seeing you.

Don't Waste a Minute!

Don't just listen to God's word. You must do what it says.

JAMES 1:22

Philip was a disciple of Jesus. One day, an angel appeared and told him to go out to a certain desert road, so Philip went. (Because that's what you do when an angel appears and tells you to do something, right?)

On that road, Philip met an Ethiopian official. He was the treasurer for the queen of Ethiopia. The official was traveling home from worshiping in Jerusalem. As he rolled along in his chariot, he read from the book of Isaiah.

When Philip caught up with him, he heard the official reading the Scriptures and asked, "Do you understand what you are reading?" (Acts 8:30).

"How can I, unless someone instructs me?" the man said (8:31). So Philip hopped up in the carriage and explained that the words from Isaiah were a prophecy about Jesus. Then Philip told him all about Jesus.

A little later, the official spotted some water and wanted to be baptized. They stopped the chariot, Philip baptized the man, and then . . . the Spirit of God snatched Philip away to preach in another town! The Ethiopian official "went on his way rejoicing" (8:39).

Not only was this great news for the Ethiopian official, but it was great news for all people. You see, under the old laws, only Jews (or those Gentiles who chose to become Jews) could be part of God's family. But Jesus came to change that. *Anyone* who follows Jesus can be part of God's family. When the Ethiopian man heard that, he didn't waste a minute! Because of his faith in Jesus, that man's life was changed forever.

Don't waste a minute either. Follow Jesus now and let him change your life forever!

Read All About It

Read more about the Ethiopian man in Acts 8:26-40.

Talk About It

The Ethiopian official didn't waste a minute. When he found out he could be part of God's family, he wanted in right away. Why do you think some people wait to choose to follow Jesus?

Pray About It

God, thank you for the gift of your Word. Please help us not just to listen to and study your Word, though. Help us to obey it too! Amen.

Let's Do This

God's Word, the Bible, is a beautiful gift to us. But we need to do more than listen to it—we need to do what it says. Is there part of God's Word that's hard for you to obey? Ask God to help you with that today.

Go Bigger

How important is it to listen and obey? Try out this tasty (or not-so-tasty!) activity to see. Grab your favorite recipe for cookies or brownies or another treat. Gather the ingredients. While a grown-up reads the instructions (and takes care of the oven parts), have everyone else work together to follow—or obey—the instructions. What would happen if you didn't follow the instructions just right?

71

Busy with Kindness

> Since God chose you to be the holy people he loves, you must clothe yourselves with tenderhearted mercy, kindness, humility, gentleness, and patience.
>
> COLOSSIANS 3:12

Peter was traveling from place to place telling everyone he could about Jesus. One day, he came to the town of Lydda. While he was there, some men from the nearby town of Joppa came to beg him for help. When Peter arrived in Joppa, the men took him to the home of a woman named Tabitha.

Tabitha (who was also called Dorcas in Greek) loved Jesus with all her heart, and she loved to serve his people. She was known for her kindness. That kindness kept her busy doing all sorts of things to help others.

When she died, many people were heartbroken. They placed her body in an upstairs room. And that's where the men took Peter.

The room was full of widows grieving for their lost friend. They showed him the coats and clothing Tabitha had sewn for them. After having everyone leave the room, Peter knelt and prayed.

When he finished his prayer, Peter said, "Get up, Tabitha" (Acts 9:40). She opened her eyes and sat up!

Through the power of Jesus, Peter had raised Tabitha to life again. Many people believed in Jesus because of her story. Her life—and death and return to life—changed the lives of so many others. And it all started with kindness.

You may be young, but you can change lives with kindness too. Start with a smile. Share what you have. Help when you can. And ask God to point others to him through your kindness.

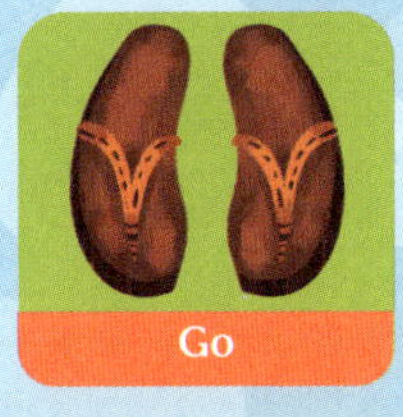

Read All About It

Read more about Tabitha in Acts 9:32-42.

Talk About It

We talk about a lot of different ways God is wonderful, don't we? Like how strong and powerful and all-knowing he is. We talk about his love and forgiveness. But we don't talk much about his kindness. How is God kind to us?

Pray About It

God, we get so busy with things that aren't important. Remind us to be busy with kindness too. Amen.

Let's Do This

Kindness is like a superpower. How can you flex your kindness superpower today? Do something for someone they can't do for themselves. Make someone's day easier. Or share with someone who can't pay you back. What kind thing will you do today?

Go Bigger

Tabitha made sure the people around her had the clothes that they needed. You can help do that too. Gather up the clothes from your closet that you don't wear or have outgrown, and donate them to a ministry that gives clothes to those in need. Choose things that will help people feel good, not clothing that's worn out or torn.

Traveling for Jesus

> Go and make disciples of all the nations, baptizing them in the name of the Father and the Son and the Holy Spirit.
>
> MATTHEW 28:19

Paul and Barnabas loved Jesus. They wanted to make sure everyone had a chance to hear about him. So they traveled thousands of miles telling people about him. Along the way, they started up churches.

None of it was easy. There were no comfy hotels to stay in. No breakfast buffets or swimming pools either. Paul and Barnabas didn't get to travel by car or zoom around in an airplane. Instead, they traveled on horses or clip-clopping camels or took dangerous boat trips. Other times, Paul and Barnabas simply had to walk. There was *lots* of walking.

Scholars think Paul traveled more than 10,000 miles during his missionary journeys. That's like traveling from Maine to California and back again—*twice*! Barnabas didn't travel quite as far, but his feet still got in plenty of miles.

Paul and Barnabas didn't let all that traveling slow them down. And they didn't let all the danger, threats, and attacks from religious leaders stop them either. They just had to share about Jesus.

What will you do to share Jesus with others? You don't have to travel 10,000 miles. Just go to wherever the people are—across the lunchroom, backyard, or ball field. You might be a little nervous at first, and it might be a little (or a lot!) outside your comfort zone. You'll definitely need some wisdom and some courage, too. But don't worry! God's got plenty to share.

And remember, every journey should start with prayer. Ask God to guide you to the person he wants you to talk to.

Read All About It

Read more about Paul and Barnabas in Acts 14.

Talk About It

Before Jesus returned to heaven, he gave his disciples a mission. It's called the great commission. You can read it in Matthew 28:18-20. Why is it important for everyone to hear about Jesus? Do you think Jesus wants you to be part of his mission? How can you share Jesus with others?

Pray About It

God, lead us to the people you want us to tell about you. Please help us to listen to their thoughts, worries, and questions. And then give us the words and the courage to share with them how wonderful you are and how much you love them. Amen.

Let's Do This

If you had a chance to tell someone about Jesus, what would you say? Think about it and practice so you'll be ready. (John 3:16 is always a great place to start!)

Go Bigger

You don't have to travel thousands of miles or climb on a camel to be a missionary. You can do it in your own neighborhood or backyard! In today's world, we often don't even know our neighbors. Start your missionary journey as a family with a get-to-know-you get-together. It could be a cookout, cookie swap, or games and lemonade on a hot summer day. Send out invitations, make the snacks, and get ready to meet your neighbors! (Don't forget to start it all with a prayer!)

A Never-Ending Love

Now we can rejoice in our wonderful new relationship with God because our Lord Jesus Christ has made us friends of God.

ROMANS 5:11

Do you ever wonder things like, *If my friends really knew me, would they still be my friends?* It's okay. We all think that sometimes. That's part of what makes God's love so great. He *does* know everything about us—every ugly thought and every selfish action. He even knows all the sins and mistakes we haven't made yet. And check this out: God knew all those things *before* he sent Jesus to save us.

That's right! God loves you so much that he sent his Son to die for you long before you ever believed in him or told him you were sorry for your sins. Jesus made a way for you to be friends with God, without requiring you to be perfect before you came to him—or even almost perfect. God loves you no matter what. *But . . .*

God won't leave you just the way you are. When you follow him, he's going to work in your heart and in your life to make you more and more like Jesus. Why? So you can be the best possible you . . . the *you* he created you to be.

Want to know one more amazing thing about God and his love? He doesn't leave you to figure it all out on your own. God sends his own Holy Spirit to live inside those who believe in him. So you never have to face one single thing alone. God is always right there with you.

That's how huge his love for you is—and it's a love that never ends.

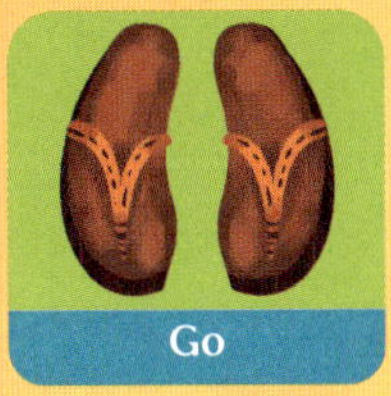

Read All About It

Read more about God's love in Romans 5:1-11.

Talk About It

In this world, so much depends on you measuring up. You've got to be good enough to get the grade, make the team, win the award. Read Romans 5:8. Do you have to worry about measuring up before God will love you? What does it mean that Jesus came to save us while we were still sinners?

Pray About It

God, help us to understand—as much as we can—just how high and wide and deep and huge your love for us is. Amen.

Let's Do This

Think about all the things you have to be "good enough" for, like sports teams, music ensembles, and honor rolls. Now think about this: God wants to give you his friendship and a home forever with him. All you have to do is love and follow him—no tryouts, no practices, no grades.

Go Bigger

Go on a BIG scavenger hunt. With a grown-up's help, go on an internet hunt to find the world's biggest . . . dinosaur, pizza, building, fish, animal, bug, toy store, star, or whatever else you can think of. Let your imagination go wild. And then remember, God's love is bigger than any of that!

Jesus Set Us Free

> Well then, should we keep on sinning so that God can show us more and more of his wonderful grace?
>
> ROMANS 6:1

In Old Testament times, there were laws about practically *everything*—what to eat, what to wear, what to do and not do—and when to do it. God gave those laws to his people to help them understand what was right and what was wrong. But no one could obey them all perfectly. It just wasn't possible.

Why? Because laws aren't able to change our sinful, selfish hearts. So even when we try to do the right thing, we can still mess up (see Romans 7:21-23). The law showed the people of the Bible—and it shows us—how much we need a Savior. And that's exactly why Jesus came.

Unlike the law, Jesus can transform our hearts! He didn't get rid of the law. He fulfilled the law by showing us how much we need him. His grace forgives us for the times we mess up and sin.

Does that mean we can do whatever we want and not worry about sin because we know we'll be forgiven? No! Sin still hurts us and others. It still pulls us away from God. Because of Jesus' grace, we get to *choose* to do what's right—not because of a law, but because we love God, because we're thankful for all he's done, and because we want to please him.

Read All About It

Read more about how Jesus frees us from sin in Romans 7.

Talk About It

In Romans 7:15, Paul says, "I want to do what is right, but I don't do it. Instead, I do what I hate." Has that ever happened to you? Maybe you got upset and said something you didn't really mean. Or you did something you knew was wrong just to fit in. What will you do differently next time?

Pray About It

God, your love and grace really are amazing. Help us use our words and actions to show how thankful we are and how much we love you. Amen.

Let's Do This

There are roughly 613 laws in the Old Testament, but Jesus summed them all up in just two: love God, and love your neighbor (see Matthew 22:37-40). How can you obey these two commandments today?

Go Bigger

The battle between right and wrong is like a tug-of-war in our hearts. Act this out with a real-life tug-of-war. Gather family and friends and divide into equal teams. How tough is it to win? Now, put everyone on one team—except one person. How much easier is it to win if you have support? That's what happens when you ask God to help you do what's right. He lends you his strength and helps you win.

75

One with God

Don't you realize that your body is the temple of the Holy Spirit, who lives in you and was given to you by God?

1 CORINTHIANS 6:19

After Jesus returned to heaven, the apostle Paul traveled to many different places telling people about Jesus and starting churches. One of those churches was located in a city called Corinth.

After Paul left Corinth to keep spreading the word about Jesus, some of the members of the Corinthian church made bad choices. These choices didn't fit with what Paul had told them, and they especially didn't follow Jesus' teachings.

They started to believe they could do whatever they wanted with their bodies. They drank too much. They were greedy with their food. And they didn't keep the promises they had made to their husbands and wives. They said it didn't matter.

A lot of people in our world today believe that too. They think they should be able to do whatever they want. But that just isn't true.

Our bodies were created by God to honor him. When we choose to love and follow him, our bodies are actually joined with God when the Holy Spirit comes to live inside us. We are "one spirit" with God (1 Corinthians 6:17)! That's an amazing gift and blessing, but it's also a big responsibility. We should use our bodies—our hands and feet, our arms and legs, our hearts and minds—to love, respect, and serve God. And when we do, he will bless us even more.

Read All About It

Read more about honoring God with your body in 1 Corinthians 6:19-20 and Romans 12:1-2.

Talk About It

When you decide to follow Jesus, your body becomes the home of God's Holy Spirit. How amazing is that? First Corinthians 6:20 reminds us that our bodies were bought "with a high price." What was that price? Who paid it?

Pray About It

God, we praise you for choosing to send your Holy Spirit to live inside us. Please help us not to forget that our bodies are your home too. Show us how we can honor you. Amen.

Let's Do This

One way to remember that the Holy Spirit is always with you is with a breath prayer. Close your eyes. As you breathe in, pray, *Thank you, God . . .* and as you breathe out, pray, *. . . for being here*.

Go Bigger

Your body is a gift, so take good care of it. Go for a family fun run (or walk) in the park. Stop by the playground to climb the monkey bars and swing on the swings. Have fun exercising and enjoying God's creation!

76

How Can You Know?

> Your love for one another will prove to the world that you are my disciples.
>
> JOHN 13:35

Following Jesus will change your life! But it probably won't happen in an instant. You'll grow a little here and a little there as the Holy Spirit works in your heart.

Sometimes, though, you'll make mistakes, and other times you'll choose to sin. Then you might wonder if you're really changing at all.

When that happens, read 2 Corinthians 3:18: "The Lord . . . makes us more and more like him." Remember that God will do what he says he will do.

But how can you know God's working in your life? First, pray and ask God to show you how he's using the Holy Spirit to make you more and more like Jesus. Then pay attention to the things you say and do.

You'll probably notice that you're kinder and more helpful than you used to be. You reach out to people you wouldn't talk to before. And when someone does something hurtful or wrong to you, you might decide not to get even but to turn the other cheek instead (see Matthew 5:39).

Maybe you don't get angry as easily as you once did. When things don't go your way, you talk to God about it instead of throwing a fit. And best of all, you want all your friends to know and love God too.

None of these things will happen overnight. In fact, you'll be working on some of them your whole life. You might shine for Jesus one day and completely mess up the next. Don't give up! God knows you aren't perfect, and he doesn't stop working on

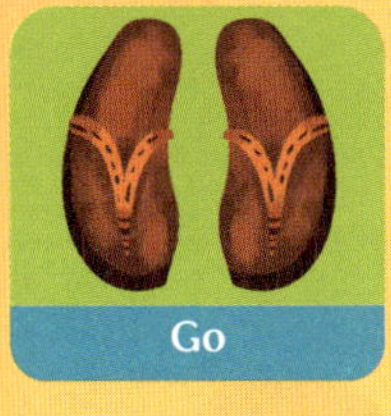

you—even if you can't see it yet. And little by little, day by day, you'll begin to see that you're living and loving more like Jesus did. *That's* how you can know that God really is working in you.

Read All About It

Read more about being transformed in 2 Corinthians 3.

Talk About It

As followers of Jesus, we want the world to know that we, well, follow Jesus! We want to act more like him and less like the world around us. What are some differences between what the world does and what Jesus would do? How can you be more like Jesus this week?

Pray About It

Father God, help us to show the world what it looks like to belong to you. Not so we will look perfect or better than anyone else, but so others will want to get to know you too. Amen.

Let's Do This

Sometimes we might think that living like Jesus needs to be big and grand for the whole world to see. But that's not always what it looks like. It can start with the person right in front of you. Listen when they speak. Offer to help. Pray for them—out loud or in your heart.

Go Bigger

Your relationship with God needs time to grow, and so do our relationships with each other. Choose a day and declare it a "No Screens Day"—no phones, TVs, or tablets of any kind. Spend the day as a family playing games, hiking, hanging out in the park, or working on a project together. And be sure to thank God along the way!

77

What Are You Planting?

> Remember this—a farmer who plants only a few seeds will get a small crop. But the one who plants generously will get a generous crop.
>
> 2 CORINTHIANS 9:6

Would you ever plant a watermelon seed and expect a coconut tree to grow? How about planting an apple seed and waiting for an orange? No way!

When we plant seeds, we expect to get what we plant. That's true for seeds . . . and it's true for a whole lot of other things too, like how we use our time, what we pay attention to, and what we do with our money and things. How we use them—or "plant" them—in the world matters.

Getting what you plant—or reaping what you sow, in Bible language—is even more true for your heart, your attitude, and the way you treat others.

For example, you can't plant gossip and snobbishness and expect to grow friendships. You can't plant selfishness and expect others to be generous to you. And you can't plant hate and expect love to grow.

So what should you do? Plant the things you want to grow. Just think about all that God has blessed you with: love, kindness, grace, and even his friendship. He hasn't given you just a little bit or been stingy with these gifts either. He's poured them out on you. When you take the blessings he's given you and pour them out—or plant them—in the lives of others, then guess what you can look forward to? A big, beautiful crop of more of those blessings both from those around you and from God.

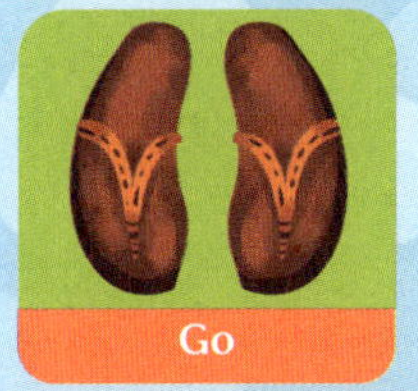

Read All About It

Read more about planting generously in 2 Corinthians 9:6-11.

Talk About It

Not only do we scatter seeds into the world with our words and actions, but we have to make sure the world doesn't scatter weeds into the garden of our hearts. What are some "weeds" you see in the world? How can you keep them out of your heart? How can you get rid of them if they sneak in?

Pray About It

God, please give us the wisdom and courage to plant seeds of your love wherever we go. And help us to keep any weeds of the world out of our hearts. Amen.

Let's Do This

Start the day by planting a "seed"—or verse—of God's Word in your heart. Keep a list of your favorite verses. Here are a few to start your garden of verses growing: Joshua 1:9, Psalm 18:19, Psalm 139:13-14, Jeremiah 29:11, and Matthew 28:20.

Go Bigger

Take a trip to the gardening shop, and pick a small plant, some soil, and a pot. Plant according to the directions, and give it the right amount of water and sunlight. Then watch it grow! Notice that if you want your plant to grow, you have to keep nurturing it with water and sunlight. In the same way, keep nurturing your relationship with God—with prayer, praise, and Bible study—so that it will also grow.

78

Grateful for Struggles?

> My grace is all you need. My power works best in weakness.
>
> 2 CORINTHIANS 12:9

Each of us can do some amazing things. We might even want to brag about some of them—like how great we are at math, basketball, or art. We aren't usually proud of the things we struggle with, though. We aren't usually grateful for illnesses, tough home lives, or learning challenges. But the apostle Paul learned to be grateful for his struggles.

Paul called his struggle a "thorn in my flesh" (2 Corinthians 12:7). Some scholars think it may have been something wrong with his eyes because he often had other people write his letters for him. But Paul never told us exactly what his "thorn" was. What he did say is that he begged God three different times to take it away.

Each time God said, "My grace is all you need. My power works best in weakness" (12:9). In other words, God uses our struggles to teach us to depend on him. And when it comes down to it, the only thing we really need is God and his grace. Not to be rich, popular, or perfectly healthy. Because none of those things last forever.

God doesn't promise us a perfect life here on earth. In fact, Jesus said we would have troubles (see John 16:33). When we trust and follow God, though, he pours his power into our lives and takes care of our greatest need—the need to be forgiven of our sins and to live forever with him.

All the struggles and tough times—sometimes he'll take them away, and sometimes he'll walk with us through them. But he'll never, ever leave us to face them alone.

Read All About It

Read more about depending on God in 2 Corinthians 12:1-10.

Talk About It

If everything in our lives were perfect all the time, we might start to forget how much we need God. How do tough times and difficulties remind us that we have to rely on God? How can our past struggles help us understand and comfort those who are struggling now?

Pray About It

God, to be honest, we would rather skip all the troubles and struggles, but we know they are part of life in this world. Thank you for never leaving us to face any of them on our own. Amen.

Let's Do This

What's something you've struggled with? How did you get through it? Be on the lookout for a way you can help someone else who has that same struggle. (For example, a fear of speaking in front of the class, or worrying about a loved one who's in the hospital.)

Go Bigger

Hospital waiting rooms are filled with people who need comforting. Find a large basket and fill it with snacks, small bottles of water, and a magazine or two. Make a card that says, "Someone is praying for you." Ask a grown-up to help you deliver them to a hospital waiting room near you.

A Way to Say Thank You

> God saved you by his grace when you believed. And you can't take credit for this; it is a gift from God.
>
> EPHESIANS 2:8

Imagine you were out riding your bike, lost control, and wrecked your neighbor's flower bed. You definitely didn't mean to, but you made a mess that needed to be fixed. Your neighbor said you owed him fifty dollars to replace everything, but you don't have that much money. So he put you to work. You pulled weeds, dug holes, and spread mulch for hours. Until you earned enough to pay him back. Whew, right?

That never happens with God. If you owed him, it would be more than you could ever pay back. Just think about it: God sent his Son for you, and Jesus died on a cross to pay for all your sins. *All* of them. *Forever.* It's impossible to pay him back for that.

Yes, the Bible is filled with instructions on how to serve God. But does that mean you have to earn God's love and forgiveness by doing all those things? No! It's not possible under your own power anyway.

Here's the beautiful part though: God knew that. He knew you could never pay him back or live without making any mistakes. He knew you could never earn your place in his family. So he offers it all to you as his gift. It's yours for free when you choose to follow him.

You can't earn God's love or grace. But when you accept these priceless gifts, you'll discover that you want to spend your whole life doing all the good things he's asked you to do. Because that's how you say, "Thank you, God, for all the wonderful things you do for me!"

Read All About It

Read more about God's gifts to us in Galatians 3:10-14 and Ephesians 2:8-10.

Talk About It

The Bible does tell us to do good works—not to earn God's love and forgiveness, but to say thank you for them. Why is it impossible to earn God's love and forgiveness? How is helping other people a way to say thank you to God?

Pray About It

Father God, you give us love and forgiveness. You never leave us, you sent your Son to save us, and you even sent your Holy Spirit to live inside us. Help us to live our whole lives saying thank you every chance we get! Amen.

Let's Do This

One of the simplest and best ways to say thank you to God is to simply close your eyes, pray, and say, "Thank you, God." Then be still and rest in the wonderful knowledge that you love God, and he loves you.

Go Bigger

Make a thank-you tree. Put a handful or two of small rocks in a large vase. Gather some branches—real or fake—and tuck them in the vase. Cut out a stack of simple construction-paper leaves. Each time you notice a gift from God, write it on a leaf. Use string, tape, or a paper clip to attach the leaves to the tree. Then watch your tree bloom with thank-yous!

80

When Did His Love Begin?

> Even before he made the world, God loved us and chose us in Christ to be holy and without fault in his eyes.
>
> EPHESIANS 1:4

It's almost impossible for us to wrap our minds around all that God knows. He knows everything—from the number of stars in galaxies we haven't even discovered yet all the way down to the details of the tiniest ant's home. He knows the birds in the sky, the flowers in the fields, and every hair on our heads.

God knows everything from every time. Which means he knew you before you were born. God even knew you before he created the world. And guess what? He loved you already—so much that he chose you and made a plan to save you many, many years before time began.

God didn't wait for you to love him before he started loving you. That's what people do sometimes: We wait for someone to love us before we decide to love them. But not God. He knew *you* and began loving *you* before he told the sun to shine. Before he ever hung the first star, planted the first tree, or taught the first lion how to roar. Before any of that happened, God chose you to be his child—and he's been waiting ever since for you to choose him back. Thank him today for choosing you.

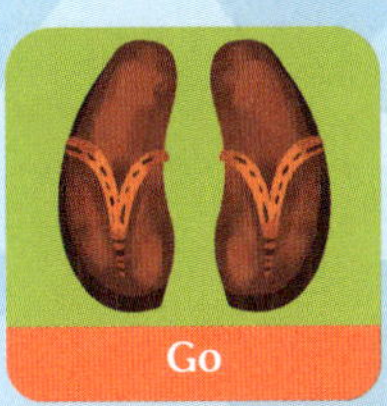

Read All About It

Read more God's love in Ephesians 1.

Talk About It

Whether you're in gym class, on the playground, or in the lunchroom, it feels great to be picked by someone else, doesn't it? Name a time you were glad to be picked.

Now remember that you have been chosen by God to be part of his family. How does that feel? Why is it better than being chosen for anything here on earth?

Pray About It

God, open our eyes to see how your mighty power—the same power that raised Jesus from the grave—works in our lives. Thank you for loving us. We love you. Amen.

Let's Do This

Choose someone today—perhaps someone you wouldn't usually pick—and invite them to join you at lunch, recess, or church.

Go Bigger

You are wrapped up in God's love—completely surrounded! Want a little peek at what that feels like? Take a big blanket and ask your mom or dad to wrap you up in it like a burrito. (Be sure you have room to breathe!) Bonus: Make burritos for dinner!

No Reason to Hide

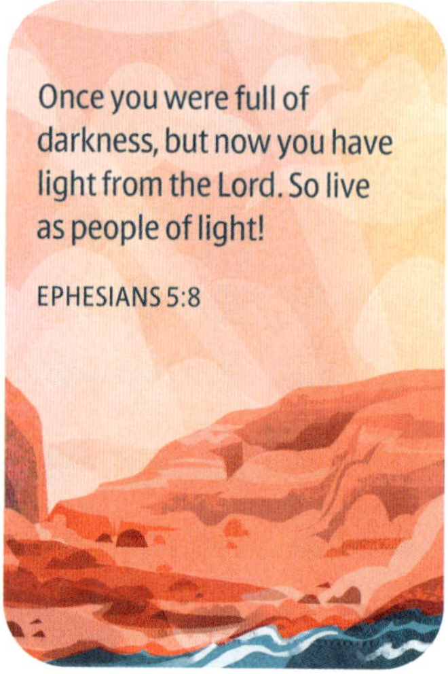

How can I hide this? Is that your first thought when you mess up? But hiding our sin is exactly what the devil wants us to do. And who wants to make that guy happy?

Here's the reason you shouldn't try to hide your sins, especially from God: because it pulls you away from him. Even if no one here on earth finds out, the guilt of knowing you messed up can make you feel like you're sitting alone in the dark.

Except you're not really alone. Guilt and shame and fear are all sitting there with you. Guilt and shame because of what you did, and fear because you're afraid someone will find out.

If you want to step out of that darkness—if you want to tell guilt, shame, and fear to get lost—there are just two things you have to do. *Confess.* Tell God you're sorry for what you've done. Yes, he already knows all about it, but he wants you to admit that it was wrong. (Don't forget to confess that you were wrong and say sorry to that person you hurt or disobeyed too!) Then *repent*, which means that, with God's help, you're going to turn away from sin and back toward God.

If you ask God to forgive you, he will. God won't turn away, and he won't say no. So there's no reason to hide.

When you confess and repent, it's like stepping out of the darkness and into the bright sunshine of God's grace and forgiveness. There's no reason to hide. Ditch the darkness and shine!

Read All About It

Read more about how to live for God in Ephesians 5:1-20.

Talk About It

Everyone messes up, makes mistakes, and sins. But what we do after that is *so* important. Think about a time you chose to do wrong—and then chose to try to hide it. How did that work out? How did you feel? What would you do differently?

Now think of a time you messed up but chose to confess and repent right away. How was that different from the time you tried to hide your sin? Why do you think God wants us to confess and repent?

Pray About It

God, please forgive us for our sins. Wash us clean, and help us to shine for you every chance we get. Amen.

Let's Do This

Take a look at Psalm 119:105. Light—the light of God's Word—helps you see the right things to do and the right way to go. Ask a grown-up to help you find a song that goes along with this verse, and use it to help you memorize its words.

Go Bigger

What is darkness? It's the absence of light. Have fun with light and dark in a game of flashlight tag. Turn out all the lights indoors or head outside at night. The person who's "it" takes the flashlight while everyone else scatters. "It" tries to tag someone by shining the light on them and calling their name. Everyone else can run, dodge, dive—but not hide—to avoid getting tagged. When a person gets tagged, they become "it."

Working for God

Work willingly at whatever you do, as though you were working for the Lord rather than for people.

COLOSSIANS 3:23

It's Saturday. You've got fun planned for the whole day, *until* . . . you remember that you have chores and a project for school and practice in a couple of hours. Do you stomp your feet? Throw a fit? Whine and complain? It's tempting to do all those things!

But what if you didn't stomp your feet, throw a fit, or whine and complain? (Does it really do any good anyway?) What if you tried something different instead?

Imagine you're working for God instead of your parents, your teachers, or your coach. Because, in reality, you are. Doing what needs to be done—without complaining—is a way to say, "Thanks, God!" for all he does for you.

That kind of thankful attitude can make the work more fun too! Instead of stomping around when it's time to tackle those chores, think of it as taking care of the home God has given you. Don't throw a fit about that project—be creative and figure out how it connects to God's creation. (For example, if you're studying oceans and waves, think about how God made the oceans—and filled them with creatures too.) And instead of whining and complaining about practice, ask God to help you do your best or show you someone on your team who needs a friend.

When you decide to do everything for God—to work for him—it has the power to turn your whole day around.

Read All About It

Read more about working for God in Colossians 3:22-23.

Talk About It

Philippians 4:4 says, "Always be full of joy in the Lord." Think of a few times when it's harder to be joyful, like when you're waiting in line or doing chores. Brainstorm ways to flip those hard times around so they become blessings instead of reasons to complain.

Pray About It

God, every moment is a gift from you. Help us to fill our moments with your joy, even when we're doing things we'd rather not do. Amen.

Let's Do This

Need a little help remembering that you're working for the Lord when you're doing your chores? Turn on some praise music or sing your own songs. Before you know it, your heart will be full of joy, and the work will be done.

Go Bigger

Tackle that big family project you've been putting off, whether it's cleaning up the yard, cleaning out the closets, or organizing the garage. Crank up the praise music, skip the complaining, and be an example of how to work for the Lord.

Pass It On!

I am not ashamed of this Good News about Christ. It is the power of God at work, saving everyone who believes.

ROMANS 1:16

Who taught you about God? Who showed you how to love Jesus—and how much Jesus loves you?

Timothy's mother and grandmother were the first to teach him how to love and serve God. Then Timothy met Paul, and Paul taught him even more about living like Jesus. Then guess what Timothy did next? He started teaching others all that he'd learned about God!

You can do the same thing. Because God is hoping you'll do what Timothy did. First, find a trusted grown-up—or a few. It might be a parent, grandparent, teacher, pastor—or anyone who will help you learn more about loving and following God. Then it'll be your turn to pass it on and teach someone else what you've learned.

And here's a hint: You don't have to wait until you're all grown up to do it. You can start sharing what you know about Jesus right now. The more you learn, the more you can share.

Will it be easy? Sometimes it will be, and sometimes it won't. There were some people who looked down on Timothy because he was younger than they were, and there are those who might do the same to you. Don't let that stop you. When you love and follow God, he plants his Holy Spirit right inside you. The Spirit will help you to be brave. He'll even help you know what words to say (see Luke 12:12)!

So you don't have to worry or be nervous or afraid. Trust God . . . and pass it on!

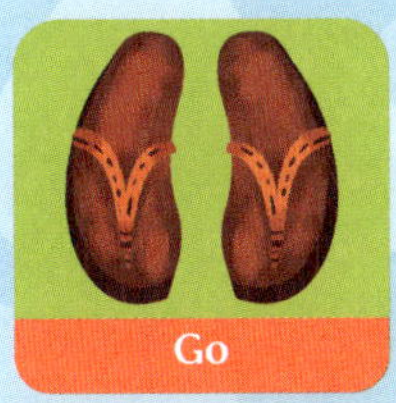

Read All About It

Read more about what Paul taught Timothy in 2 Timothy 1.

Talk About It

Second Timothy 1:8 says, "Never be ashamed to tell others about our Lord." Have you ever been ashamed or embarrassed to talk about God? What made you feel that way? How could you find the courage to be bolder? What would you do differently next time?

Pray About It

God, please forgive us for the times we hesitate to share about you because we're worried about what others might think or say. Help us to be brave and bold and tell others about you when you give us the opportunity. Amen.

Let's Do This

Who are the people who've helped you learn to love God? Next time you see them, say thanks and give them a hug.

Go Bigger

Paul told Timothy not to let anyone look down on him because he was young but to be a good example for other Jesus followers (see 1 Timothy 4:12). Be a good example by teaching a Bible lesson of one of your favorite stories. Teach it to your family or to a class at church. Use puppets or act out the story yourself!

84

Best Book Ever

> All Scripture is inspired by God and is useful to teach us what is true and to make us realize what is wrong in our lives.
>
> 2 TIMOTHY 3:16

There are about a gazillion books in the world—give or take a million or two. There are adventure books packed with prison escapes and shipwrecks, mystery books where detectives search for clues, and books about love and friendship and daring to do what's right.

Did you know that the Bible has all those kinds of stories? Adventures, prison escapes, shipwrecks, mysteries, love, friendship, and daring—they're all in there! And did you know that they're all 100 percent true?

There's no other book in the world like the Bible. What makes it so special? The Author! Its words are *inspired*. That means that even though people wrote down the words, it's God who gave them the message. So every word is true. Every word can teach you what's right and what's wrong and how to stick to what's good. It's packed with promises—about who you are, who God is, and what he will do. And you can know that God will keep each and every one.

The truths you find in the Bible are your sword to fight off the evil one. They're your hope on hard days, and they're your joy every day. The Bible is God's gift to you. Read it and believe it, and it will transform your whole life!

Read All About It

Read more about God's Word in 2 Timothy 3:14-17.

Talk About It

The Bible is the most wonderful and amazing book. It's so powerful because it's alive and working in our lives! Read Hebrews 4:12. What does it mean that God's Word is alive? How does it work in our lives? Why is it important to know God's Word?

Pray About It

God, thank you for the gift of your Word, the Bible. Please make our hearts hungry to read it so that we can grow closer and closer to you. Amen.

Let's Do This

In sports, teams sometimes have winning streaks, which means they just keep on winning. Start your own winning streak with the Bible. Read at least one verse a day—or more! How many days in a row can you go? How long will your winning streak be?

Go Bigger

Have a family Bible reading time at least once a week. After you've read a passage, invite each person to share the words, phrases, and ideas that jumped out at them. Write them on a whiteboard or poster board. Talk about what they mean. Then brainstorm ways to apply what you've learned from them to your lives. (The Gospels—Matthew, Mark, Luke, and John—are a great place to start!)

85

Absolutely Everything

Let us come boldly to the throne of our gracious God. There we will receive his mercy, and we will find grace to help us when we need it most.

HEBREWS 4:16

What if someone knew absolutely everything about you? Every word you said, every thought that zipped through your mind, everything you did—and *everything you hid!* Guess what? God does.

God knows that secret you never told anyone. He knows what you did when you thought no one was looking. And he knows the truth behind that lie you told. Don't worry, though. That's a good thing. A very good thing. Because God already knows absolutely everything about you, you don't have to try to hide anything from him. (It's impossible anyway.) He's ready to listen. That's not all—it gets even better. Because Jesus came to live here on earth and was once a kid too, he understands what it's like to be tempted. Next time you want to do something you know is wrong, remember that Jesus can relate. (The difference is that he never gave in—and he'll help you say no to temptation too!)

No matter what you do, God still loves you, and he wants to hear from you. That's why he's sent you an invitation. It's right there in his Word in Hebrews 4:16. Take a second and read it again. God wants to talk to *you*. But God doesn't want you just slipping in to talk to him, or sneaking in, or worrying whether or not he has time to see you. He wants you to come to him like you belong there. Because when you love and trust in Jesus, you become part of God's family . . . and with him is exactly where you belong.

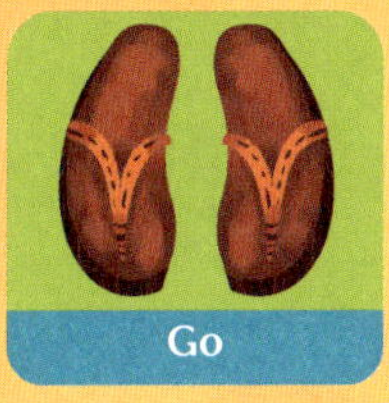

Read All About It

Read more about talking to God in Hebrews 4:14-16.

Talk About It

Name some of the most important people in the world, like presidents, kings and queens, and celebrities. Could you just pop in and chat with them any time? Now, talk for a moment about who God is—the Ruler of everything! How wonderful and amazing is it that he invites you to talk to him anytime and about anything?

Pray About It

God, you invite us to step into your throne room and talk to you. That's just so amazing, and we're so grateful. And here we are, God. We want to talk to you about _____. Thank you for listening. Amen.

Let's Do This

Jesus was once exactly your age. He struggled with the same temptations and challenges you do. And he did it so he would be able to understand and help you. Think about what a gift that is as you go through your day today. Pray about the big and small challenges you're facing, knowing that Jesus understands it all.

Go Bigger

What would Jesus do? Gather as a family and name one temptation you struggled with this week. Ask the group, "What would Jesus do?" Brainstorm a few different answers. Then look up Bible stories and verses to see if you got the answers right.

A Little Trouble

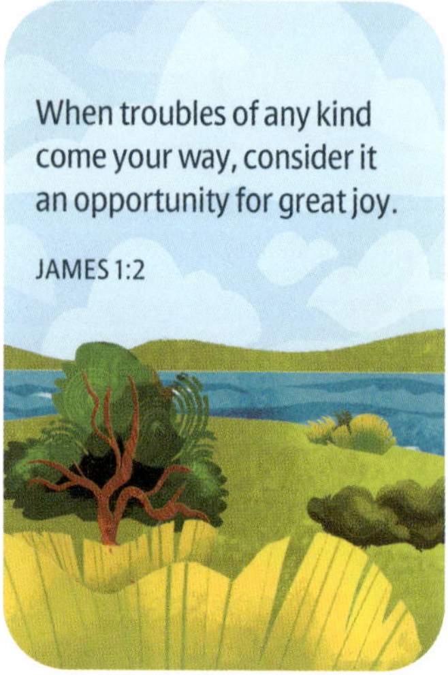

Wait! Read that verse up top again. Troubles and great joy in the same sentence? How is that possible?

Nobody likes troubles. They're no fun. They mess stuff up. And they're . . . *trouble.*

James, the guy who wrote the book of James, isn't saying that troubles themselves are anything to be joyful about. Rather, he's saying they create an *opportunity* for joy.

How? By giving you an opportunity to grow. Not taller, but stronger in your faith.

Imagine you had to move and start all over in a new city, church, and school. That would be troubling, right? But you decide to trust God and see what he will do. So every day you talk to him and ask for help.

God might first give you the courage to walk into that new school. Because that would be tough, right? Next, he might send a friendly teacher your way. After that, he might nudge another kid to invite you to sit at their table for lunch. Soon you feel right at home. You realize you really can trust God to help you.

Knowing that you can count on God pours joy and peace into your heart.

Then, the next time any trouble comes along, you'll know exactly what to do. Talk to God. Because you *know* he'll listen and help you. Your faith in him has grown stronger.

And it all started with a little trouble.

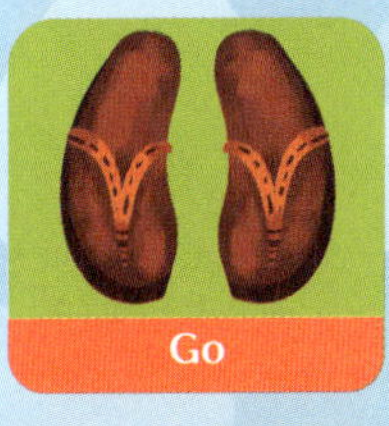

Read All About It

Read more about troubles in James 1:2-4.

Talk About It

James 1:3 says, "When your faith is tested, your endurance has a chance to grow." What is endurance? How could troubles both test your faith in God and help your faith in God to grow? What could help you stay focused on God when you're struggling with a problem?

Pray About It

God, when troubles and problems hit our lives, it's not easy to see the joy. Teach us how to look for all the ways you're loving and helping us. Because that's always a reason for joy! Amen.

Let's Do This

Is there a trouble you're facing right now—big or small? Ask God to show you how he's using it to help you grow.

Go Bigger

Struggle through this egg race! Give each person a spoon and a real or plastic egg. Decide on a course for racers to follow. Each person must balance their egg all the way to the finish line. If they drop it, they must go back to the start. Make it more troublesome by having them walk backward. Cheer each other on! And remember, when life is full of struggles and troubles, God is cheering you on.

87

You've Been Chosen!

> You are a chosen people. You are royal priests, a holy nation, God's very own possession. As a result, you can show others the goodness of God, for he called you out of the darkness into his wonderful light.
>
> 1 PETER 2:9

How amazing does it feel to be chosen? Maybe you were picked to play on the team, to star in the play, or to be first in line. Whether it's for a huge award or to be the first to lick the cookie-dough spoon, there's just something that feels wonderfully good about being chosen.

And there's also something that feels horribly awful about *not* being chosen. The fact is, there will be times when you won't be chosen. Because not everyone can be chosen for everything. But the evil in this world will try to tell you it's because you're not good enough, not smart enough, or not *something* enough.

Don't listen, and here's why. There are zillions and zillions of things in this world that you might or might not be chosen for. But there's only one thing that really matters. And you've already been chosen for that.

You've been chosen to be part of God's family. All you have to do is say "Yes!" and choose him back. When you do, you'll be wrapped up in love and mercy, and you'll be forgiven for every sin. You'll get to tell others about him. And best of all, you'll know he's always with you—no matter what.

All because you've been chosen.

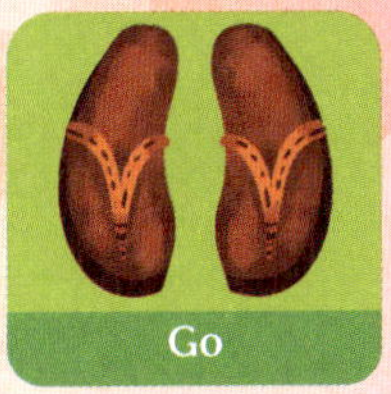

Read All About It

Read more about being chosen in 1 Peter 2:9-10 and 1 John 3:1-2.

Talk About It

God is the King of all creation. When you turn away from sin and follow him, he adopts you into his family. You know what that means, right? You become his royal child—a prince or princess in God's Kingdom! How does it feel to be part of God's royal family? How should knowing that you're his change the way you act? The way you treat others?

Pray About It

Father God, you've chosen us to be your very own children. Thank you! Please help us show others how to become part of your family too. Amen.

Let's Do This

When the world starts telling you that you aren't good enough or that you don't really matter, close your eyes. Then whisper the truth to yourself: "I am chosen by God."

Go Bigger

If you're royal, then you need a crown, right? Cut out strips of poster board—enough for everyone to have a crown. Decorate with designs, stick-on jewels, or whatever you like. Tape or staple the poster board into a circular crown. Then gather everyone for a royal portrait—wearing their crowns, of course.

88

Everything You've Got

> You must love the LORD your God with all your heart, all your soul, all your mind, and all your strength.
>
> MARK 12:30

What happens when cold things, like ice cream, warm up? Or when hot things, like french fries, cool off? How do they taste? Not so great, right?

That in-between stage—neither hot nor cold—is called *lukewarm*. Food isn't the only thing that can get lukewarm. Our faith can too, and Jesus says that's no good.

People with a lukewarm faith know God is real, but they don't care enough about him to really change their lives for him. They might obey him, if it's something they wanted to do anyway. They might praise him, if they feel like it or if it will make them look good in front of others. They don't think they need God to save them.

Jesus spits out lukewarm faith like lukewarm fries. If you want to keep your faith "hot," you need to love, trust, and follow God with everything you've got!

What does it look like to worship God that way? It's loving him with all your heart, soul, mind, and strength. It's putting him first in your time and your heart, not last. It's praising him because he's worthy, not because you want to look good. It's knowing that you need him and obeying him because you trust that he wants only the best for you. And it's being willing to tell the whole world—or at least your little corner of it—about what he's done for you.

Don't let your faith cool off. Keep it hot by loving God with everything you've got.

Read All About It

Read more about how to avoid having a lukewarm faith in Revelation 3:15-19.

Talk About It

God commands us to love him with all our heart, soul, mind, and strength (see Deuteronomy 6:5 and Matthew 22:37). What would that look like on an ordinary Tuesday, at church, at dance practice, or in the middle of a ball game? Brainstorm ways to show your love for God with your heart, soul, mind, and strength.

Pray About It

God, your love for us is amazing and endless. Teach us to love you with our whole selves. And please give us the courage to share our love for you with others—with everything we've got! Amen.

Let's Do This

Challenge yourself to show your love for God in these four ways today: with your heart, soul, mind, and strength. Be creative. Can you pick two of the ways, or three, or all four?

Go Bigger

Have a "lukewarm" taste test with an ice cream sundae night. Start with some just-starting-to-melt ice cream. (Don't eat if it's been sitting out more than fifteen minutes!) How does it scoop? Does it stay on the cone? Do the sprinkles slide right off? It's not great, right? Kind of like lukewarm faith. Now dive into some frozen ice cream with all your favorite toppings!

89

All Together

> I saw a vast crowd, too great to count, from every nation and tribe and people and language, standing in front of the throne and before the Lamb.
>
> REVELATION 7:9

In our world today, people are often separated into different groups. They're separated because they live in different countries or have different cultures. Maybe they dress differently or speak another language or have a different color of skin.

You might see it happen around your school or with your friends. The athletes hang out with other athletes. The science kids are in one group while the theater and band kids are in another. Oh, they might mix a little bit now and then, but sooner or later they separate again. And then there are the kids who are left out—they don't seem to fit in with any group.

One day all that will change. When Jesus returns to earth, all the people who love him will be gathered together. No one who loves and follows God will be left out of his Kingdom.

It won't matter what clothes they wear, what sports they play or don't play, or what color their skin is. It won't matter if they speak English, Chinese, Spanish, or Swahili.

In God's Kingdom, there will be people from every nation and every tribe, from all over the world. His praises will ring out in all the different languages as God's people come together to worship him.

This has been God's plan since before time began, and one day, Jesus will come again and make it happen.

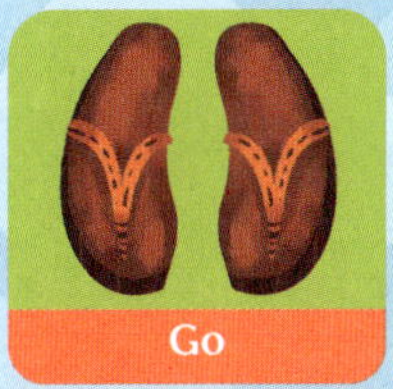

Read All About It

Read more about Jesus' return and God's Kingdom in Galatians 3:28-29 and Revelation 7:9-10.

Talk About It

Revelation 7:9 says our new life with God will be filled with people "from every nation and tribe and people and language." God doesn't judge us by where we're from, what we look like, or how much money we have. He only cares that our hearts love him and love others. How different is that from the way our society judges people? How wonderful will that be?

Pray About It

Father God, your Kingdom will be the most amazing place to be. Thank you for sending Jesus to make it possible for us to live with you there forever! Amen.

Let's Do This

Listen to—and even learn—a praise song in another language (maybe even sign language). You might not recognize the words, but you'll be able to recognize the love behind them.

Go Bigger

As a family, visit a Christian church from another culture. (Check their website or call ahead to see if they have any special notes or requests for visitors.) What do you notice that's different from your own church? What do you notice that's the same?

90

Jesus Is Coming . . . but When?

> Jesus has been taken from you into heaven, but someday he will return from heaven in the same way you saw him go!
>
> ACTS 1:11

After Jesus rose from the grave, he stayed on earth for another forty days teaching his followers before he returned to heaven. He promised that he would be back one day. *But when?* his apostles wanted to know.

That's the question we want answered too, isn't it? But only God the Father knows the answer (see Matthew 24:36). Jesus said he would come like a thief in the night (see Matthew 24:43), not to steal, but to give his people life forever with him. But we must stay alert and always be ready for his return.

How do we stay ready? By keeping our hearts and minds focused on God. By loving others. By sharing God's truth so others will be ready too.

So why doesn't God just go ahead and tell us when Jesus is coming? He has plenty of reasons. One is that God wants us to trust him even when we don't understand or know the exact answer. Another reason is that if people knew the exact day Jesus was coming back, many would wait until the last minute to start following him. They'd keep doing whatever they wanted, disobeying and ignoring God. They wouldn't choose him until they had no other choice.

God wants everyone to choose to be part of his family *now*. He wants everyone to follow him and to start loving and caring for each other *now*. There's no reason to wait. We can follow God right away and be part of his family while we wait for Jesus to return.

Read All About It

Read more about Jesus' return in Revelation 19:11-16.

Talk About It

Name some times you have to wait in your life. How can you wait well—instead of whining or spending too much time on screens? Only God knows when Jesus will return, so we don't know how long we'll be waiting—or if he'll return in our lifetime. How can we wait well for Jesus? (Hint: God tells us in Matthew 22:37-38).

Pray About It

God, we know Jesus is coming, and it will be the most amazing day! Help us to stay alert and ready, and help us to wait well. Amen.

Let's Do This

Let yourself stare up at the clouds as you imagine that one day Jesus will return through those clouds (Acts 1:9-11).

Go Bigger

Have a "Coming in the Clouds" picnic. Grab blankets, and maybe a snack or two, and head outside. Stretch out and gaze up at the clouds. What shapes do you see? A lion? A boat? An elephant balancing on a ball? Then talk about how one day Jesus will come through the clouds, and we will meet him there and live with him forever (see 1 Thessalonians 4:16-17).

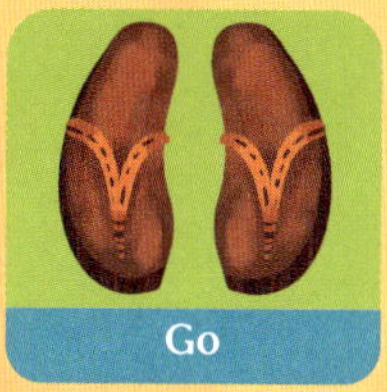

About the Author

Tama Fortner is an ECPA Award–winning and bestselling author with more than sixty titles to her credit, as well as a contributing writer to the *GO Bible*. Her latest releases include *Prayers for Each Moment*; *God, I Feel Sad*; and *God, I Feel Scared*. She is the writer behind the million-selling *Indescribable Kids* series with Louie Giglio, as well as a number of books in the *Jesus Calling* children's line, including the wildly successful *Jesus Calling: 365 Devotions for Kids*. Tama has collaborated with such well-known authors as Max Lucado, Levi Lusko, and Sadie Robertson Huff to create inspirational books for all ages.

Tama began her writing career at the ripe old age of eight when—aspiring to be like her favorite literary heroine, Jo from *Little Women*—she set up a cardboard desk in her bedroom closet. Since first putting pen to paper, she has never tired of the scritch-scratch of the pen or the clickety-clack creations of the keyboard.

In addition to her books, Tama has written articles and devotions that have been featured in numerous publications, including *Woman's Day*, Crosswalk.com, and the *Jesus Calling* blog. She has been a guest on television's *Today in Nashville*, as well as numerous podcasts.

Tama and her husband have two all-grown-up-now children who are living their best lives with those they love. When not busy with words, she dabbles in watercolors and loves teaching little ones about Jesus. Tama lives on the outskirts of Nashville, Tennessee, with her family and two feisty little pups who are convinced they're people too. Learn more at tamafortner.com.